POLAR BEARS
The Arctic's Fearless Great Wanderers

ANTHONY DALTON

VICTORIA · VANCOUVER · CALGARY

Heritage House Publishing Company Ltd.
www.heritagehouse.ca

Library and Archives Canada Cataloguing in Publication
Dalton, Anthony, 1940–
  Polar bears: the Arctic's fearless great wanderers / Anthony Dalton.

ISBN 978-1-926613-74-1

  1. Polar bear. I. Title.

QL737.C27D35 2010   599.786   C2010-904734-6

Series editor: Lesley Reynolds.
Proofreader: Karla Decker.
Cover design: Chyla Cardinal. Interior design: Frances Hunter.
Cover photo: A polar bear at Churchill, Manitoba. HuntedDuck/iStockphoto.

 The interior of this book was produced using 100% post-consumer recycled paper, processed chlorine free and printed with vegetable-based inks.

Heritage House acknowledges the financial support for its publishing program from the Government of Canada through the Canada Book Fund (CBF), Canada Council for the Arts and the province of British Columbia through the British Columbia Arts Council and the Book Publishing Tax Credit.

13 12 11 10   1 2 3 4 5
Printed in Canada

For Mike Warburton:
a fine researcher and a good friend

Author's Note

To ensure consistency with historical accounts and to avoid confusion, the author has used imperial measurements throughout this book.

Contents

Prologue

ALTHOUGH HER NAME TRANSLATES INTO *English as*
Greyhound, the Dutch exploration ship moved slowly
through the patches of broken ice, her captain and pilot seek-
ing the safest route to the east. Greyhound *had sailed north*
from Amsterdam, crossed the Arctic Circle off Norway's west
coast and rounded the top of Scandinavia in the Barents Sea.
For weeks she had followed veins of open water, within sight
of land, reaching for the channel between Novaya Zemlya
and Vaygach Island.

With only two sails set to catch the wind, she looked
untidy—undressed—but it was safer that way. On her deck,
sailors on watch studied the floes that surrounded them and
prayed the ship would get through without being holed. With

the ice concentration getting thicker, pilot Willem Barentsz called for the two sails to be furled. As the ship slowed to a stop, he ordered the anchors to be set into a large floe of grounded ice close by. It would make a reasonably safe anchorage until the wind changed and moved the ice away from shore.

The sailors had been cooped up on board for weeks as the expedition worked its way through the Arctic ice in search of a navigable northeast passage across the top of Russia. While the ship was anchored to the ice, Barentsz and the expedition's commander, Jacob van Heemskerke, allowed a few men to go ashore at a time to stretch their legs, unaware that extreme danger lay not far away.

Two sailors walked together, happy to be off the ship and enjoying walking on the land again, despite the snow underfoot and the cold air. They smoked their pipes and chatted about home, about their wives and children.

Out of sight of the ship, hunting seals from the ice floes packed against the shore, a polar bear sniffed the air and sensed fresh meat. Standing tall on its hind legs, it saw two creatures some distance ahead. To the bear, they looked like big seals. It dropped to all fours and set off in pursuit.

Hungry and too skilled at the hunt to make a mistake, the bear crept stealthily toward the creatures. Using the rafted ice to shield itself from sight, it crawled on its belly over the snow-covered open ground to get close, staying downwind so its scent would not scare its prey into sudden escape.

The two sailors, oblivious to everything except their

conversation, walked at a casual pace. Behind them, unseen by any on board the ship or on the shore, a huge white bear rose up from the snow and padded a few feet closer. Within striking distance of the men, it raised its front legs and massive forepaws and spread them wide. Its mouth gaped open, showing a fearsome array of teeth, and it lunged forward.

Introduction

THERE ARE EIGHT MAJOR SPECIES of bears in the world, and with one exception, they live in the northern hemisphere. At the top of the list is the magnificent polar bear, one of the largest bear species in the world and the largest terrestrial carnivore. The polar bear is known by a variety of popular names: nanook, nanuq, nanuk, ice bear, sea bear, eisbär, isbjørn, Arctic bear and white bear, and to scientists as *Ursus maritimus* (formerly *Thalarctos maritimus*). The great yellowish white bears roam the Arctic ice in pursuit of seals and the tundra in search of anything else edible. They also occasionally stray far to the south, way below the Arctic Circle, where and when conditions permit.

The other species of bears live in a great variety of

habitats. The Asian black bear (*Ursus thibetanus*) is found in northern Iran, across the mountainous areas of Afghanistan, Pakistan, India, throughout the Himalayas and as far east as Japan. For the most part, it lives in forested mountain terrain above 13,120 feet. Its diet is primarily nuts and shoots, olives, figs and insects. The endangered and shy giant panda (*Ailuropoda melanoleuca*) lives in the wild only in a few parts of China. Easily identified by its black and white colouring, it is a herbivore and quite harmless. The brown bear (*Ursus arctos*) ranges across northern Eurasia and North America. A subspecies, the grizzly bear (*Ursus arctos horribilis*), is found in the northwestern quarter of North America as far north as the Arctic. It will eat almost anything and can be extremely aggressive if threatened. The North American black bear (*Ursus americanus*) is widespread across Canada and Alaska and found in many other American states. It inhabits forests and, like its grizzly cousin, will eat just about anything edible from vegetation to deer. A herbivore, the spectacled or Andean bear (*Tremarctos ornatus*) is the only bear to be found in the southern hemisphere. It lives in the Andes mountain range from Venezuela to Chile. The sun bear (*Ursus/Helarctos malayanus*) is a native of Malaysia that lives in tropical rainforests and eats plants, nuts and small animals.

Each species of bear has its own peculiarities and its own folklore and devotees. None, however, can equal the great polar bears for their mystique, their skills, their ability to fascinate humans and their single-minded determination to survive.

It is probable that the grizzly bear was the first Arctic bear. Over the last 200,000 years or so, those that strayed north adapted colouring and physique to match the northern environment. In doing so, the grizzly of a long-gone era has become the formidable polar bear. They are now found throughout the Arctic from Siberia to Alaska, across Canada's northern Yukon, Northwest Territories and Nunavut, plus most of Greenland and the Norwegian islands of Spitsbergen. Although polar bear tracks have been seen in the vicinity of the North Pole, experts believe that most bears remain a few degrees to the south, where the ice breaks and they have a greater opportunity of finding food. Polar bears are also found all around Hudson Bay, on the shores of Manitoba, Ontario and Quebec. In fact, Ontario's polar bears live so far south of the Arctic, along the southwestern shore of Hudson Bay and throughout James Bay, that at the southernmost extremity of their range, they are on the same latitude as Kamloops, British Columbia, and Calgary, Alberta. The only other area where polar bears roam far to the south of the Arctic Circle is between Alaska and Siberia. When winter conditions freeze the Bering Sea, sometimes as far as 50 miles south of the Bering Strait, the polar bears often follow to find seals and walrus at the edge of the ice mass.

Scientists estimate that there are approximately 20,000 to 25,000 polar bears in the world. Of those, the majority, believed to be some 15,000 individuals (at least 60 percent of the total), roam Canada's vast North.

Male polar bears usually weigh up to 1,540 pounds, and the females can reach well over 800 pounds, although the latter tend to peak at about 600 pounds. The largest male polar bear on record weighed in at an impressive 2,204 pounds. A typical male will measure between 6.5 and 8 feet from the tip of its nose to the end of its stubby tail. Some, of course, are a little smaller and a few are considerably larger. Females are usually about half the size of males. In the main, once they reach maturity, they are all big, and they move fast on land, on sea and on ice.

Polar bears appear to have yellowish white fur. In fact, the millions of hairs that make up their thick coats are a perfect camouflage to suit the Arctic's white landscape. The bear's black skin is designed to absorb any heat available, typically keeping it up to 15 degrees Celsius warmer than the surrounding air temperature. They have long, non-retractable black claws, dark brown eyes and dark blue or black tongues. Under the skin is a thick layer of fat that does double duty as an effective insulation against the cold and a store of usable energy.

Aboriginal cultures consider polar bears to be wise as well as powerful. The Inuit recognize the species as superior hunters and have always understood and appreciated the bears that roam the land on which they live. The Inuit are also the first people to recognize the gradual reduction in bear populations as greenhouse emissions and other pollutants tarnish the environment beyond repair. Today, because of its potential plight, the mighty Arctic bear has become a symbol of creatures threatened by climate change in the Arctic ecosystem.

Polar bears are wild creatures, and they are not easily frightened. They are curious, and therefore they are dangerous. Yet a study of fatal polar bear attacks on humans in the wild showed that only eight people were killed by polar bears in Canada in the past 30 years. In Alaska, during the same period of time, only one person was killed, while five people were killed in Spitsbergen. In the many decades since records have been kept, only 19 people have died from confrontations with polar bears in Russia. In Churchill, Manitoba, where polar bears are regular visitors to the town and a mainstay of the tourism infrastructure, only two residents have been killed by bears since the early 1700s. However, none of those figures make polar bear encounters any less dangerous.

The more inquisitive the bears become, added to their apparent complete lack of fear when confronting an adversary, the more dangerous they will be. A hungry bear will attack and kill a human if the need for self-preservation or food arises. In all instances in Canada and Alaska, and probably in Russia too, where a human was attacked and killed by a polar bear, the bear was either thin and hungry or deliberately provoked. Potentially fatal encounters between humans and polar bears will almost certainly increase as the sea ice melts and the hungry bears, unable to hunt seals, are forced to hunt onshore.

1

The Last
Great Nomads

WATCHING A POLAR BEAR LOPING across the tundra, stalking a seal or using its powerful forepaws to drive it through frigid waters from one large piece of icy, floating real estate to another is like watching a perfect hunting machine in fluid action. A polar bear on the move personifies arrogance, relentlessness, exceptional energy and extreme danger. The great Arctic bears are at the apex of the northern food chain, and their primary focus is on catching and eating other creatures, preferably ringed seals, their favourite food. They also eat bearded seals, harp seals, walrus, beluga whales, narwhals, seabirds and their eggs, and occasional carrion. According to one report, a couple of bears were discovered dining on a recently released but perfectly preserved

350-year-old whale carcass that had been entombed in ice for generations.

Through the long process of evolution, nature has endowed the Arctic bears with a phenomenal sense of smell, said to be 100 times more sensitive than that of humans. One polar bear was tracked travelling in a straight line for 40 miles over rafted ice and patches of open water to where a seal rested out of the water. Researchers believed the bear had smelled the seal on the ice over that vast distance.

Polar bears show great skill and ingenuity when hunting. Typically, bears plunge headfirst into water from ice floes, but they can be stealthy when necessary. There are stories of bears showing remarkable foresight during a hunt. Seeing a seal on an ice floe, a bear was observed turning its back and lowering itself, one hind leg at a time, into the water in order to avoid making a splash and alarming the seal. It then swam underwater and burst up right beside the startled seal, which had no chance to escape.

Some bears have been known to swim under the ice toward a seal's breathing hole when the seal is relaxing on the floe close by, then come up through the hole quickly so the seal has nowhere to go. Bears also will make their way through thin ice toward their prey by swimming on their sides. Using one forepaw on top of the ice and the other below, they pull themselves along, moving quickly and without much noise.

A *National Geographic* video shot in the Canadian

Arctic shows a polar bear stalking a ringed seal. The bear is on the ice. The seal, weighing more than 100 pounds, is swimming underneath. The bear knows where the seal is, but the seal, which must come up to breathe, is unaware of the danger above. As the seal comes up through a hole in the ice, the polar bear launches itself directly at the opening. The force of its leap, with four legs at full stretch, almost causes the bear to somersault over the hole as it thrusts its forepaws, head and shoulders down to grab the seal. A few seconds of wild wrestling ensues before the bear drags its prey onto the ice and runs away with it to dine.

The stalking ability of polar bears is extraordinary to watch. On rocky Southampton Island in northern Hudson Bay, a bear was seen studying a herd of walruses sunbathing on weather-worn granite. Walruses are the most dangerous of polar bear prey because of their lethal tusks. On this occasion, the bear had the advantage of altitude, watching the walruses from above. Instead of launching itself into the potential banquet and risking the wrath of a multitude of massive ivory tusks, it made its way over the rocks to the sea, keeping downwind of the walrus herd.

At the shore, the bear slid carefully into the water and swam with only nose, eyes and the top part of its head visible. Abreast of the walruses and still downwind, it pulled itself ashore and shouldered its way into and through the herd to reach its chosen victim: a walrus pup. The mother tried to protect her offspring with flashing tusks, but the bear knocked her aside with a hefty blow. As the herd scattered, intent on reaching the safety of the sea, the bear tore into the pup. None of the old bull walruses, which were sunbathing on a ledge above the action, took any notice. Within a few minutes of the attack, even the cows and their calves in the sea had settled down.

Polar bears also show remarkable strength and skill in hunting beluga whales. Churchill resident and noted wildlife photographer Mike Macri owns Sea North Tours. He takes visitors out in his large jet boat, *Sea North II*, to watch whales in the estuary and to search for polar bears on the drifting ice in the bay, as well as on the smooth, flat rocks along the coast. Mike relates a story that explains the enormous strength of a healthy polar bear. A bear was seen patrolling the south side of the Churchill River when it suddenly lunged at a passing young beluga. The bear was quicker than the beluga. It hooked it with its long claws and threw the heavy creature up on the shore behind it.

Mike Macri's story is far from unique. Far to the north of Hudson Bay, where Cunningham Inlet cuts into Somerset Island, beluga whales congregate in large numbers each summer. They travel there to get into two streams of warmer water, where the females give birth. In shallow waters and within easy reach of land, they can become prey for wandering bears.

A young beluga found stranded on the beach in Cunningham Inlet carried deep parallel scars down its back,

When they are not hunting for food, polar bears often indulge in play-fighting. These two were photographed at Churchill, Manitoba.
MILA ZINKOVA

almost certainly from an attack by a polar bear. Experts noted that the attack probably happened when the beluga surfaced close to an ice floe where a bear waited. However, bears have been known to target beluga whales in their natural domain, particularly when the whales surface in small areas of open water with ice all around. Three belugas were killed by bears near Grise Fiord on Ellesmere Island in the early summer of 1979. A polar bear in the Russian Arctic was seen to lay flat on the ice and smack a surfacing beluga on the head to stun it before hauling it out onto the ice.

Polar bears are magnificent hunters, but they are opportunists as well. A report from Churchill told of three juvenile belugas held captive in a large tank. A polar bear attacked and pulled at least one of the whales out. Then, in a frightening display of strength, it dragged the hapless beluga some 75 feet across the ground. The whale weighed 594 pounds.

When hunting or in danger, adult bears can move with exceptional speed, considering their size. Young bears are even more agile than their parents. After their mother was shot, two bear cubs chased on a Greenland shore scaled a 60-degree incline on a glacier at speed and without a pause. They then made their way over large crevasses, still at full stride. When cornered by Inuit dogs higher up, one was shot by hunters, but the other escaped by climbing an almost vertical snowy crag and disappearing over the other side.

William Scoresby, an 18th-century English navigator and whaling captain with vast experience in sailing Arctic waters, told the wonderful tale of a bear that was able to spring a simple rope trap three times in succession and walk away with the bait. He explained that sailors placed a rope noose on the ice with some *kreng*, or cooked whale meat, in the middle to attract a bear. When one came along, it got its foot caught in the noose but soon removed it with its other front paw and took the bait. The sailors tried again, and the same bear came back. It pushed the noose aside and walked away with the food. A third attempt was made by burying the noose in crusty snow. Once again, the bear returned. It sniffed around the buried noose, pulled it out of the snow and tossed it aside. The bear ran off with its latest snack and did not return.

Not all heroic attempts to escape by captive bears were successful. Scoresby's men shot a sow and captured her two cubs. They kept them on the main deck of their sailing ship most of the time but did allow one to go for a swim while tethered. The cub immediately swam to an ice floe and tried to flee. The rope held it back. Then the natural intelligence of the young bear took charge. Scoresby wrote:

> Near the edge of the floe was a crack in the ice, of considerable length, but only eighteen inches or two feet wide, and three or four feet deep. To this spot the bear returned; and when, on crossing the chasm, the bight of the rope fell into it, he placed himself across the opening; then, suspending himself by his hind feet, with a leg on each side, he dropped his head and most of his body into the chasm, and, with a foot applied to each side of the neck, attempted for some minutes to push the rope over his head. Finding this scheme ineffectual, he removed to the main ice, and running with great impetuosity from the ship, gave a remarkable pull on the rope; then, going backward a few steps, he repeated the jerk. At length, after repeated attempts

to escape this way, every failure of which he announced by a significant growl, he yielded himself to his hard necessity, and lay down on the ice in angry and sullen silence.

These incredible creatures also have developed specialized architectural skills. Females build dens for themselves when pregnant, and they spend months tucked away from the outside world. They instinctively understand the need for temperature regulation and adequate ventilation, and they know how to accomplish that by poking paw-sized holes in the roofs of their chambers. All polar bear dens feature these necessities. In winter, the dens are carved out of snowbanks and sometimes have multiple chambers, either side by side or one above the other. In summer, particularly along the southwestern shores of Hudson Bay, the bears excavate earth dens above the permafrost. These seasonal tundra dens offer the bears protection from the summer heat and the hordes of mosquitoes that infest the region.

Polar bears rarely attack humans, but will do so if threatened or hungry enough. Without the lethal weaponry mankind has devised, such as high-powered rifles, a polar bear would win over a man every time. Author and Arctic veteran Duncan Pryde looked at it from a different perspective. He wrote, "The rifle, properly handled, makes man the most powerful animal on earth. No animal, no matter how cunning or strong, can do anything against a rifle." He was right, of course. Even so, the reality is hardly sporting.

The Last Great Nomads

These supremely confident Arctic predators are the last great land nomads on this planet. Human nomads trek across great deserts and through deep jungles. They sail across the seven seas, but they can't equal the apparently erratic wanderings of polar bears. Individual bears have been known to travel vast distances on land in the course of a year, and they have been recorded swimming for many hours at a time for long distances—as far as 62 miles from any land or large drifting ice floes. Polar bears have a unique style of swimming, using only their powerful forepaws. They hold their hind paws and legs out straight and use them as rudders. Despite only using their forepaws, they can maintain a steady speed of 6.2 miles per hour. When swimming underwater, as they do when stalking seals, the bears' nostrils close tightly, enabling them to stay submerged for two minutes at a time. One bear tagged by scientists is known to have walked and swam across the Arctic as it hunted, taking a year to cover over 1,990 miles.

Ten separate female polar bears were captured along the north Alaskan coast at different times. Scientists placed collars equipped with telemetry transmitters around their necks and then freed the bears and tracked their subsequent movements by satellite. The bears left their often-overlapping prints on the polar ice between points from Herschel Island, Yukon, and along the Alaskan north shore to Point Barrow and south on the sea ice to Norton Sound, off the village of Kivalina. At least one of them roamed far across the Chukchi

Sea, west as far as Wrangel Island, near the Siberian coast, and hundreds of miles north into the barren, jumbled ice of the Arctic Ocean. They all travelled enormous distances during the year or so that the collars remained attached. The collars are no impediment to the bears and automatically fall off after a maximum of about two years. Only female polar bears can be collared; male bears have necks that are wider than their heads, so the collars simply fall off.

A single adult female bear collared and tracked for two years from Polar Bear Provincial Park in Ontario roamed as far east as the Belcher Islands, west beyond the Manitoba border and far out onto the sea ice of Hudson Bay, tracing zigzag lines for a few thousand miles.

Polar bears depend on sea ice for their survival. For them, the ice floes are hunting stations and breeding sites, and they are an integral part of the polar bears' lives. Sea ice is not just frozen water. Living within its frozen mass are algae and phytoplankton, sustenance for zooplankton and crustaceans that in turn become food for Arctic fish, seabirds and seals. Polar bears fit into the Arctic's natural hierarchy far above these creatures, but the bears cannot survive without them. Ringed seals are the bears' favourite food due to their high fat content. Polar bears prefer fat because, scientists believe, they digest it more easily than protein. Despite that preference, they are adaptable. In Spitsbergen, resident polar bears have been reported as being "adept at catching reindeer" and eating them. To stalk a reindeer and bring it down would require a careful mix of cunning, stealth, speed and strength, and that capability is a solid testament to their natural abilities. When hunters from Inuit villages along Alaska's Beaufort and Chukchi seas bring home a bowhead whale, polar bears soon collect to dine on their share of the abandoned carcass. In Churchill, Manitoba, the bears are happy to snack on waste food at the town dump.

As the ice retreats earlier and earlier each year, the polar bears' hunting season is reduced accordingly. That forces bears ashore sooner and away from their preferred food sources. An additional two weeks without ice from which to hunt can cause as much as an 8 percent weight loss in an adult bear. With each additional week that the seas remain ice-free, that weight loss is magnified and the danger to polar bears becomes more and more critical.

Polar bear scientist Dr. Ian Stirling amplified that concern when he wrote, "For every week earlier that [ice] break-up occurs in the Hudson Bay, bears will come ashore roughly 10 kg lighter and thus in poorer condition. With reproductive success tied closely to body condition, if temperatures continue to rise in response to increases in greenhouse gas emissions and the sea ice melts for longer periods, polar bear numbers will be reduced in the southern portions of their range and may even become locally extinct."

Dr. Stirling was writing about the potential fate of polar bears in southern Hudson Bay and James Bay. There, the sea ice is melting earlier each season and freezing and forming

Two polar bear cubs shelter in a snow den, where they live with their mother for the first few months of their lives. US FISH AND WILDLIFE SERVICE

later in the autumn. Similar ice conditions are occurring in western Hudson Bay. Those areas are, of course, far south of the Arctic Circle, but the situation is showing signs of deteriorating quite rapidly in the Far North also. Ships navigating between Canada's High Arctic islands find their routes blocked with less and less ice with each passing year.

In a May 2002 description of the Arctic, Jennifer Morgan, director of the World Wildlife Fund's Climate Change Program, wrote of its most important resident, "This is the kingdom of the polar bear—an ambassador for arctic nature and a symbol of the impacts that global warming is increasingly having around the world."

There are 20 identified Arctic and subarctic areas containing polar bear groupings. All are congregated around the north polar ice cap, on the shores of Russia, Norway, Greenland, Canada and Alaska. They are home to anywhere from less than 200 individuals in the smallest area—Norwegian Bay, in the Canadian Arctic islands—to as many as 2,500 to 3,000 in the largest areas—Lancaster Sound in Canada and the Barents Sea, between northern Scandinavia and Russia. Southern Hudson Bay, including James Bay, has been reported to have from 500 to 1,000 individuals. Western Hudson Bay is estimated to have similar numbers.

Although their far-ranging travels are motivated by the need for food or a mate, polar bears appear to enjoy their nomadic lives. The males spend most of their lives travelling. Both male and female bears are superb natural navigators. Arctic ice is constantly on the move, following a roughly circular pattern around the north polar regions. It is almost featureless, and what variations there are change quickly and often in response to winds and sea currents. Yet female polar bears, known as sows, roam far and wide on that same ice for months at a time and then somehow find their way back to traditional denning sites with unerring precision. When they enter their dens, they will remain inside for anywhere from four to eight months. Cubs are born between November and January, and the sows alternately nurse their young and sleep. In the spring, in late March or early April, the sows and cubs emerge together for the first time. They stay close to the den, however, and sleep there at night for the initial 12 days or so. As soon as the mothers feel the time is right, usually when the cubs are about three or four months old, she will take them hunting on the sea ice.

The males, which habitually stay out on the ice throughout the winter, also have acutely developed internal guidance systems. They too can find their way back to favourite sites without fail.

2

On Spitsbergen and Points East

OBLIVIOUS TO THE BITING COLD, a polar bear padded restlessly across the bleak island off the north Russian seashore. Blocked by large mounds of rafted ice on the land, it took to the sea, where the Arctic Ocean was littered with drifting floes of ice carved by nature into irregular shapes and sizes. Leaping gracefully from one floe to another, swimming when necessary, it was constantly on the lookout for seals, preferably fat young ringed seals. On the shore, the bear had left deep, plate-sized paw tracks in the fresh snow. After a winter of solo nomadic wanderings, without much sustenance, the bear was thin and in need of nourishment. As it foraged for food, its thick, warm, yellowish coat rippled over its body and legs, looking several sizes too large, as if it needed the attention of a good tailor.

Not far away, the white sails and tall masts of the *Winthont*, or *Greyhound*, a Dutch exploration ship searching for a safe route through the Northeast Passage, showed occasionally over the chaotic masses of ice. On the afterdeck, pilot Willem Barentsz watched the ice, the sky and the few patches of open water as his ship ghosted through the maze of narrow channels between the ice floes. Seeing the way ahead blocked, he ordered the two remaining sails furled, and anchored the ship to a substantial acreage of stationary grounded ice. After a brief discussion with the expedition's commander, he called to the mate, "Let the men off watch go ashore for a few minutes, if they want to, in pairs and only a few at a time."

Two men scrambled off the ship. They were laughing and happy to be free of its confines, even for a short while. None on board or on the ice had seen the polar bear between them and the nearby land. None knew of the tracks left in the snow.

The bear, oblivious to the presence of the ship due to the direction of the light breeze, continued its quest for food. Then a sudden wind shift changed the scene. An acrid smell of a living creature and warm blood filtered along the shoreline on the clean Arctic air. The bear stopped and wrinkled its black nose, searching for the source. Raising its elongated head, it stood up tall on its hind legs, and its keen dark eyes scanned the distance, focusing on two indistinct shapes up ahead on the land. To the bear, the shapes represented seals. It dropped to all fours and began to stalk its quarry.

The two sailors from the Dutch expedition ship talked quietly to each other as they stretched their legs. After many weeks at sea, the walk onshore felt good. Neither of them had any idea they were being followed by a fully grown, hungry and extremely dangerous predator.

The bear moved in silence, employing its instincts to take advantage of the cover afforded by blocks of rafted ice. To cover open ground, it slithered on its belly to keep its profile as low as possible. When it was only a few paces behind the men, it stood up, stepped forward with fore-paws extended and wrapped one of the men in a crushing embrace. Unaware of the bear's presence, he thought one of his sailing companions was fooling with him. He called out in annoyance, telling his assailant to leave him alone. Beside him, his companion looked in horror and shouted, "A bear!" With that, he ran back toward the ship to warn the rest of the crew and to get help.

Polar bears do not give up their prey easily, and this hungry bear probably had little or no experience with man-kind. It killed the man and began to devour him. When the crew arrived on the scene, armed with muskets and pikes, the bear left its kill and attacked another man. The rest of the sailors fled in panic, leaving their shipmate to his fate.

After awhile, three of the braver men went back to

This artist's rendition of Dutch sailors from the Heemskerke-Barentsz expedition of 1596 shows them defending themselves from a polar bear attack in Arctic Russia. GERRIT DE VEER, *THE DIARY OF GERRIT DE VEER*, 1596

the scene and killed the bear with their pikes. They then retrieved what was left of the two unfortunate sailors for burial under whatever rocks they could find, as it was difficult to dig a grave in the frozen ground. With the interment out of the way, they skinned the bear for its pelt and the meat it could provide. When stretched out, the pelt was a full 13 feet long.

Willem Barentsz and his crews had many close encounters with polar bears. On one of his three Arctic voyages, which took place in 1594, 1595 and 1596, Barentsz's sailors captured a polar bear after hitting it several times with musket balls but without apparently injuring it to any great extent. All they managed to do was to slow the creature down and make it angry. Keeping it at bay with pikes, they managed to get a noose around its head, planning to tow the injured bear behind their rowing shallop to the mother ship. The polar bear had other ideas. Instead of struggling to escape once it was in the water, it climbed over the stern and joined the sailors in the small boat. Unluckily for the bear, the rope noose caught on the rudder. It held fast long enough for the frightened crew to stab the angry bear to death with their spears.

Off a cape near the Arctic islands of Novaya Zemlya, just north of the Russian mainland, Barentsz moored his fogbound ship to a large berg of floating ice, intending to wait for better visibility. Barentsz wrapped his cloak around himself to ward off the cold damp air. He stamped his feet to get some life into them and walked back and forth, willing the fog to clear. While pacing the deck, he heard an unusual noise and, looking over the side, discovered a polar bear attempting to climb on board. When Barentsz sounded the alarm to call all hands to the deck, the men made so much noise the bear retreated for a while. It soon returned and made another attempt to get aboard the ship. Barentsz ordered the crew to fire, and the combined effects of four guns sent the bear running far from the noise.

Only a few weeks later, still in the Northeast Passage and trapped by ice for the duration of winter, some of Barentsz's crew were attacked by three bears at once while they were building a hut on land. Running as fast as they could, the sailors made it back to the ship. They were chased by the bears, which also clambered on board. One of the crew grabbed a halberd (a long pole with an axe and a spike at its head) and thrust it into the mouth of one of the bears, sending it off the ship in pain and panic. The other two bears followed their startled and injured companion immediately.

After a discouraging winter spent trapped in the small hut onshore, the crew were delighted to see the sun return for a few minutes on January 27. With the sun came the polar bears again. One was so determined to get at the food it could smell that it tried to break down the door to the hut. When that failed, it climbed to the roof and attacked the chimney, roaring with anger as it did so. It was unsuccessful, but there were more scares to come. A bear came close enough to a guard that the frightened man smelled its breath. He was one of the lucky ones, escaping with his life.

Six decades later, in 1668, another Dutch captain, Kees de Jonge, and members of his whaling crew were paddling or rowing two small boats when they saw a polar bear on the shore. Captain de Jonge attacked the bear with his lance and inflicted a severe wound to its stomach area. Convinced the bear could not survive more than a few minutes, de Jonge followed it, expecting it to fall and die any moment. Then he planned to take its pelt. The bear, however, was tougher than the Dutchman realized. When it understood it could not escape, it climbed a rock, turned to face the captain and launched itself into the air.

With blood streaming from its wound, the heavy bear covered 26 feet and landed on top of the surprised Dutchman, knocking him down. Captain de Jonge dropped his lance when the bear hit him. With no weapons, he was completely at the mercy of the bear's wicked teeth and claws. Kees de Jonge, however, was lucky that day: one of his men distracted the bear long enough for the captain to get to his feet and run for safety.

Year after year, the unpredictable Arctic continued to create hazards for explorers, whalers and the like. In 1743, 14 Russian walrus hunters heading for the main island of Spitsbergen were blown off course by a powerful storm that damaged their rudder. Unable to steer the ship, they fetched up in the heavy ice surrounding the island of Edgeøya, south and east of their intended destination. Four of the men managed to cross from ice floe to ice floe to reach shore to look for a hut that one had heard of from other Arctic sailors. When they returned from their successful quest, they found a change in the wind had cleared the bay of ice. There was no sign of the ship or the 10 men left aboard. In fact, no trace of them was ever found. The ice, responding to the fresh offshore wind, had begun to move and had almost certainly crushed the hull and sunk them.

For the next six years, the four men survived on the otherwise uninhabited and barren island under extremely hostile conditions. Only three species of mammals exist on the islands that make up the Spitsbergen archipelago: reindeer, fox and polar bear. When the ice breaks up in summer, however, the seas are busy with seals, walrus and fish. For the beleaguered sailors, there was little they could do at sea without a boat. Life would have been desperate enough without the resident polar bears. With them—and Edgeøya has the largest concentration in the Spitsbergen group— the men were at risk from attack every day. Two of them attacked and killed a polar bear with a pair of homemade spears early in their solitude. Over the next six years, they killed nine more bears that attacked them. The men were finally released from the isolation when a ship, also blown off course by a storm, happened by in the summer of 1749 and saw a signal fire.

It wasn't just Dutch explorers and Russian sailors who tangled with polar bears. Men from other nations had their heart-stopping moments too.

Captain James Cook was the greatest navigator in the world in his time and perhaps the greatest navigator of all time. In 1788, also on Spitsbergen, Cook had a much-too-close encounter with a polar bear. He was attacked onshore,

A Norwegian road sign on Spitsbergen warns of the presence of polar bears. STATENS VEGVESEN VEGDIREKTORATET/NORWEGIAN PUBLIC ROADS ADMINISTRATION

and like others before him, wrapped up in a bear's embrace. The great captain was saved by the calm attitude and accurate shooting of his ship's surgeon, who put a bullet in the bear's head.

Captain William Scoresby, who wrote of many encounters

with bears and whales in the Arctic, told of a bear getting too close for comfort, again in the Spitsbergen region. The crew of one of his small whaleboats attacked a polar bear that fought back and climbed aboard their boat. The sailors threw themselves into the icy waters and hung on the gunwales while the bear took over. It sat there in the stern of the boat, like a captain, until the crew of another whaleboat shot it.

Spitsbergen's polar bears have, perhaps justifiably, earned a reputation for malevolent behaviour. In 1977, an Austrian camper was attacked at Bay of Madeleine. The bear killed him with a single blow. Ten years later, two Germans came under attack on the island of Edgeøya. They both survived, but one lost his scalp and the other received savage bites to his arms and legs.

Another visitor, Eric Giuglaris, was asleep in a cabin when a bear came calling at 5:00 a.m. He said, "I was awakened by the explosion of a pane of glass—and I mean explosion! The bear, stuck by his great size in the window casing, held himself a meter and a half away from me, his head in the center of the window." Giuglaris fired two rifle shots over the bear's head at close range, but to no effect. The bear stayed where it was and stared at him. It took two more shots, this time from a flare gun, before the bear could be convinced to go away.

Twenty-six polar bears were killed on Spitsbergen between 1987 and 1992. Fifteen of those were killed in self-defence, and twelve were the result of bears getting too close to tents or cabins.

A news story out of Spitsbergen in 2008 recounts the ability of polar bears to use camouflage as a weapon. Two women hiking alone walked toward a hummock of snow. One of them thought she saw it move slightly but then decided she was mistaken. She passed it without giving it additional thought. It was just a snow mound. As her companion drew level with it, the snow hummock exploded into action. The bear inside launched itself into the air and hit the woman hard, killing her instantly. It then ripped her body apart while the first woman looked on in fear and horror. She recovered before the bear took any notice of her and ran back to camp to warn others in her party. It was much too late for the woman who had been attacked, and it was too late for the bear, which was shot.

In July 2010, two Norwegian men attempted to circumnavigate Spitsbergen in kayaks. They were attacked by a polar bear while camped onshore in their tent. One of the men was dragged about 130 feet from the tent and badly injured. The bear was hunted down and shot.

3

To Greenland
and Arctic Canada

FAR WEST OF SPITSBERGEN, GREENLAND and the maze of Canada's Arctic islands provide the main land masses in the north polar ice cap. Both areas are well-known polar bear habitats, each with sizable populations. Whalers and explorers in those regions often found themselves in violent confrontation with hungry bears.

In May 1818, Captain Hawkins, in charge of the whaler *Everthorpe*, chased a whale from one of his whaleboats north of Davis Strait off the west coast of Greenland. A polar bear came alongside, and Hawkins stabbed it in the chest with a lance. Reaching up, the bear clawed Hawkins off the boat and tossed him into the sea. While the boat's crew hauled their bleeding captain back aboard, the bear escaped without further assault. If it hadn't been for the proximity of Captain John Ross' two expedition ships, HMS *Isabella* and HMS *Alexander*, which happened along soon after, the injured man might have died. Instead, he was attended to by a naval surgeon from one of Ross' ships and survived to hunt whales again.

Ross and his men spent four years in the Arctic and became used to seeing polar bears and the results of the predators' actions. The fleet's surgeon repaired what remained of a leg of an Inuk who had been so badly mauled by a bear that his Native companions cut off the injured leg below the knee and stitched up the stump as best they could. A ship's carpenter carved a wooden leg to replace the lost limb.

In 1850, the British steam-powered ship HMS *Intrepid* was working north through heavy ice in Baffin Bay, en route to Lancaster Sound to search for clues to the disappearance of the Franklin expedition of 1845. Some of the crew attempted to kill a polar bear while out bird hunting in one of the ship's boats. Armed with a shotgun loaded with No. 4 birdshot, they saw a bear on an island and gave chase. When one of them fired, the bear, which had been hunting seals, reacted predictably to being peppered by small metal pellets. It got mad and, according to one of the men, "He growled and trotted around the island." They continued to fire load after load of the almost-useless birdshot in the bear's direction, hitting their target repeatedly. Tiring of the onslaught of miniature missiles, the bear plunged into the sea and swam for patches of broken ice, climbing onto one. Its tormentors followed in their boat. They had exhausted all the birdshot and were reduced to shooting a waistcoat button or two. When that failed to have any effect, one of the sailors broke the blade off his knife and rammed it, broken end first, into the muzzle of his gun. Surprisingly, it worked when he pulled the trigger, although it did not add significantly to the bear's wounds. By this time, the only weapons left were the oars and a couple of boathooks. Excited though they were at the sight of the furious bear prowling the ice and leaving a trail of blood, the men understood that the contest was over. The wounded and angry but no doubt relieved bear slid into the water and made its escape.

Two other sailors from *Intrepid* were chased by a bear a few weeks later. They managed to row fast enough to outdistance their pursuer and regain the mother ship safely. There was an element of comedy about this crew's adventures with polar bears. The general incompetence of the sailors in dispatching their prey would have been funny if the potential consequences had not been so serious.

As 1850 drew to a close with the expedition still in the Arctic, somewhere in the region of eight bears, singly and in pairs, approached the ship over a short period of time. Only one of them, however, gave up its life. The rest must have felt themselves extremely fortunate to have been the moving targets of a host of supremely indifferent marksmen. There were additional hazards for the men too. It was not unusual for sailors to be mistakenly shot at by their own companions while out patrolling the ice for bears. Three of *Intrepid*'s officers proved to be no more skilled at the hunt than their men. They fired at a sow and her cub. Two of the guns misfired, while a shot from the third injured the young bear. Then the situation descended into farce.

Lieutenant Sherard Osborn, plus a few other men, set off on foot across the ice to kill the bears. They followed them to an island, where the bears shinned up a steep cliff and looked down on the sailors milling about below. Osborn's gun failed to fire time after time. The sailors urged him on, convinced they would soon get the bears. All they had between them for weapons was the lieutenant's gun, which would not fire, and a single snow knife made from old iron. They weren't equipped to fight anything dangerous, let alone two bears, one of which was wounded, but the men wanted to try anyway. Fortunately for them, their young officer had more sense and called for a withdrawal to the ship.

The various searches for the missing ships of Sir John Franklin's Northwest Passage expedition contributed to the deaths of many polar bears. Lieutenant Leopold McClintock of the Royal Navy went out in command of the 177-ton screw-yacht *Fox* on behalf of Lady Franklin. In April 1859, after spending the winter trapped in ice on Baffin Bay, the ship was finally released and crossed the Arctic Circle, heading south. The crew saw three polar bears in one day, but they were too far away to hunt. Then, a day or two later, in McClintock's words, "Today a fine bear came within 150 yards [of the ship] and was shot by our sportsmen." The crew must have hauled the carcass on board, probably for the pelt and perhaps for the meat, because McClintock described the size and condition of the bear's paws.

Johann Miertsching was a Moravian missionary travelling with Robert McClure's force, which was searching for evidence of the Franklin expedition from the Bering Sea end of the Northwest Passage. Miertsching reported a distressing polar bear attack on an Inuit child near Cape Bathurst. The child's mother was collecting shellfish on the shore while the infant played with pebbles nearby. "She heard [the child] scream and [saw] a polar bear was dragging the child off in its jaws, gripping it pitilessly with its fangs; he swam off to a piece of ice, and the poor bereaved mother saw how the savage beast tore and devoured her beloved and only child." The bear almost certainly saw the child as a seal and acted according to its instincts.

McClure's men saw polar bears regularly and almost always shot at them. Sometimes they were successful, often not. There was one humorous episode regarding a bear sighting. Distances in the clear Arctic air can be extremely deceptive. Creatures quite close up can appear to be much larger animals far away. On one occasion, the distinctive form of a bear was seen on the ice, and a party of sailors set off to kill it. They plowed through slushy snow and loose ice to within a couple of hundred feet of the "bear" when it suddenly flapped its wings and took flight. Instead of a polar bear, the men were pursuing a snowy owl.

Charles Francis Hall's 1871 expedition on board the American steam sailer *Polaris* set off for the region of the North Pole and, not unexpectedly, became trapped in ice in a small harbour on Greenland's west coast. In the summer of 1872, *Polaris* was freed, though damaged, and sailed for the south. The ice closed in again and held the ship tight for two months. In the second week of October, a gale broke the ship free but separated the crew into two groups. Fourteen men on board sailed away at the whim of the storm. Nineteen men, women and children were left on the ice to fend for themselves. They drifted on the ice for the next six months. They all survived the ordeal and were picked up by another ship, but they had a few anxious moments due to polar bears.

In one instance, two of the ship's huskies attacked a bear while out hunting on the ice with crew members. One dog suffered "several severe blows" from the bear. Although injured, it recovered. Its companion also got the worst of the fight. The bear lashed out, hit the dog and hurled it against a block of solid ice. The men were convinced the dog was dead and so left it there. Meanwhile, one of them dispatched the bear with a carefully aimed shot. One day later, the dog left for dead limped into camp and subsequently recovered from its unequal bout. The bear, which had won the battle against the dogs but lost against the men, fed the sailors with juicy steaks for a few days.

Two young polar bears roam on the rocky tundra shores of Hudson Bay, waiting for the ice to return. MIIA "MYRTTI" RANTA

A Danish research ship, the schooner *Dagny*, with a company of 16 young men—sailors, scientists and naturalists—sailed out of Copenhagen in June 1920 to spend a year on the east coast of Greenland. Only a few weeks later, the small ship was crushed by massive ice, and the crew had to spend the next year fending for themselves on an inhospitable and uninhabited coastline. Polar bears became a problem. Even before the ship's loss, the team had to be careful because of the threat they posed. Marius Madsen, a 19-year-old naturalist, wrote of being out on the ice pack: "Whenever we were away from the ship, we were in ever-present danger from roving polar bears."

The ship's experienced skipper, Captain Hansen, was hunting ptarmigan with Madsen when the two separated briefly. Hansen climbed a ridge of rock and came face to face with an approaching polar bear. He let off a blast with his shotgun, but the pellets did nothing to deter the bear. It kept on coming and was only a few feet away when the captain finally got his rifle levelled. He fired at the head, which he could almost touch, and the bear dropped dead. On the way back to the ship, the men captured two polar bear cubs and took them back to the ship on leashes. They were intended to be sent to zoos, but the ship's sinking changed all that.

Prior to the sinking, two separate parties of three men each had been deposited onshore to begin their work. One of the men, Tutine, was an artist. With him was his pet poodle. Alone and distant from the camp, Tutine had placed his shotgun on the ground and moved some distance away to set up his easel to paint a mountain scene. As he was sketching the outline of a nearby cape, he noticed a polar bear approaching. It was obviously interested in him and much too close. Tutine made two fatal mistakes. His gun was too far away to reach quickly, and he ran for all he was worth. With his dog beside him and the bear in pursuit, he raced toward his weapon. Bears can run faster than men, and this one was no exception. When Tutine reached his gun, the bear was almost on him. Before he could raise the barrel and fire, the bear crushed his head. The poodle must have fought the bear in defence of its master, because it later staggered back to camp badly injured and had to be shot.

Eight weeks into the expedition, *Dagny* became trapped in heavy ice about 30 miles off the Greenland coast. Due to the severe damage she suffered, Captain Hansen ordered everyone onto the ice, taking all possible supplies for an extended attempt at survival. The two polar bear cubs so recently captured had to be shot. Within three hours, the ship had sunk. The crew made their way across the ice to Shannon Island, where four of them lived in abandoned huts and continued their work. The others went farther, to Bass Rock, where there were more old huts, and worked from there. One year after *Dagny* sank, her survivors were rescued by men from another scientific research ship.

During that long wait, bears became a regular menace. Madsen was working alone in a shack on Bass Rock, not far from the island. Waking from a deep sleep in the night, he heard the by-now-familiar howling of the wind, combined with an unusual sound coming from the door. Poorly fitted, the door was open very slightly, and the black snout of a polar bear poked through the gap. Madsen found the situation amusing, as well as alarming. Convinced the bear could not get into the hut, his sense of humour took over.

"I tickled his nose with my finger. He became curious again, and pushed his snout through the crack, and again

I tickled it." Madsen went through this dangerous game half a dozen times until the bear tired of playing and went off to inspect another shack. Madsen dressed and went out with his rifle. Holding the weapon in one hand and the door in the other to keep it from banging in the wind, he found himself staring at a bad-tempered female—the same bear whose nose he had so recently tickled. The bear roared at him, and he fired twice from the hip. One shot went between the bear's eyes and the other into its heart. It dropped like a stone. It is unlikely that Madsen ever took liberties with a polar bear's nasal organ again.

In 1967, American adventurer Ralph Plaisted put together an expedition to travel across the polar ice cap from Ellesmere Island in Canada's Arctic in an attempt to reach the North Pole by snowmobile. Although the expedition fell far short of its objective, the team experienced the Arctic in its many moods. They also had the expected confrontation with a polar bear, though without undue stress on either side.

The bear was feeding on a seal and seal pup it had just killed when one of Plaisted's team saw it from a distance of no more than 30 yards. The men and their dogs made so much noise that the bear abandoned its freshly caught meal and made itself scarce among the pressure ridges. The expedition members missed an opportunity for a close-up view of a polar bear. They were disappointed, but perhaps they were luckier than others who have strayed too close to the Arctic's largest and most dangerous carnivore.

4

Arctic Slaughter

THE EARLY EXPLORERS OF THE ARCTIC and the later whalers who decimated the leviathans of the seas soon learned that inquisitive polar bears were easy prey for their firearms. They shot or lanced every bear they saw for two very basic reasons: because they could, and as a form of self-defence to prevent attack. There are no records of how many bears died under those misguided actions. But the explorers and whalers weren't alone in their wanton destruction of Arctic and subarctic wildlife. Commercial hunters had completely wiped out the population of polar bears on St. Matthew Island in the Bering Sea by the early years of the 20th century.

The Englishman Martin Frobisher made three voyages to the subarctic. On his third expedition in 1577, while in a strait later to be named after Henry Hudson, a party of 20 of Frobisher's men chased a large polar bear. Most bears will flee from trouble if possible. This one apparently did not understand that unwritten rule. It proved to be an exceptionally aggressive member of its species and fought back with great valour. The armed men won, despite the bear's best efforts, and dined on juicy steaks for some time afterward, but the fight could have had a much more serious outcome.

In 1585, in the Elizabethan era of sea exploration, Captain John Davis, who would become a brilliant British navigator experienced in voyaging the northern seas, sailed up the east coast of the land mass we know as Baffin Island in search of a northwest passage. Davis commanded two small expedition ships, and he and his crews of 42 men saw their first polar bears on land while sailing into a bay that the captains named Exeter Sound, a name still found on maps today.

The two ships, *Sunshine* and *Moonshine*, left the port of Dartmouth in southern England on June 7. Contrary winds made the North Atlantic voyage difficult and slow. Although the first half of the crossing was of little interest due to the winds, the second half certainly made up for it. They saw a "very great whale" on July 6 and more on a daily basis. Then, "on the 16th, 17th and 18th we saw great store of whales."

Neither ship was equipped to hunt the gigantic sea mammals, so they left them alone. It's just as well they did, because they were reaching an area of extreme danger for the two small vessels. On July 19, they were confused to find themselves being set northward on a fast-moving tide for a short distance. That changed quite abruptly to what the log recorder referred to as "a very calm sea, which bent to the south-south-west. Here we heard a mighty great roaring of the sea, as if it had been the breach of some shore, the air being so foggy and full of thick mist that we could not see the one ship from the other." The two captains knew that the ships were close together, but they were invisible to each other.

Captain Davis and two other men took a small boat and went to investigate. It wasn't long before they learned the reason for the strange conditions. Hidden in the mist was much drifting ice. They were almost certainly among the ice floes of the southern reaches of the east Greenland current. The noise was that of the waves breaking on the floes and the ice grinding and crashing together. The two ships turned south, then west, and then north again, working up what is now Davis Strait toward Baffin Island.

On August 6, they anchored in Exeter Sound, under the shadow of Mount Raleigh. On the shore, four white shapes drew their attention. Some thought they might be goats or wolves. A crew set off on the hunt, but they were surprised at what they found closer in: "When we came near the shore we found them to be white bears of a monstrous size." The bears were big, but the men needed fresh meat, so they went on the attack with muskets and pikes. John Janes, who wrote the account, said, "My piece [a musket] was charged with hail-shot and a bullet. I discharged my piece and shot him in the neck; he roared a little, and took the water straight, making small account of his hurt." Undeterred and determined not to lose him, they followed in the boat and finished off the job with boar spears. They also killed two more bears that night.

The next day they happened on a much larger bear asleep on the top of an island just offshore from Mount Raleigh. The men shot it several times, but it fought back with great courage, eventually escaping into the water of a small cove. There they had it trapped and soon put an end to its misery. When Janes measured the bear's forepaw, he found it to be 14 inches in breadth. That bear must have been huge, because a 12-inch span is at the top end of the scale. Bears use their large paws to distribute their weight better when walking on thin ice.

John Davis never did find the Northwest Passage, but his three Arctic expeditions paved the way for all those who followed in his quest.

Danish sea captain Jens Munk left Copenhagen in 1619 in command of the frigate *Unicorn*. In company with another ship, the sloop *Lamprey*, he crossed the Atlantic to search for a northwest passage to China. They ended up in what is now Hudson Bay and sailed west-southwest to arrive at the mouth of the Churchill River. Curious about the beluga whales that swam in the estuary, Munk harpooned one from a small boat and pulled it in to shore to examine it. Afterward the carcass was left there, high and dry, even though its meat could have fed the ships' crews. A polar bear soon scented the dead whale and stopped to feed on the unexpected bounty. Captain Munk killed the bear with a single musket ball. Inexplicably, having chosen not to eat the small white whale, the crew instead dined on the bear. What they did not know was that polar bear liver is extremely toxic. Some of the sailors ate liver as well as the meat and died as a result.

Occasionally, polar bears benefited from the wanton killing of other animals. Victorian-era Arctic explorer and yachtsman Bernard Leigh Smith wrote of a Norwegian expedition from August 1852 that landed a group of 16 men on High Rock Island, in the Spitsbergen group. They are said to have killed so many walruses, leaving the carcasses piled high on the rocks, that many more of the creatures were trapped and also fell prey to the sharpened lances of the attacking men. By the end of the slaughter, 900 walruses had died. There was no possibility that the few men could carry such a bounty home, so hundreds of dead walruses were left on the island with their skins and tusks intact. Polar bears, blessed with their superior sense of smell, soon crossed the ice and sea to feast on the largesse.

Two decades later, another Norwegian expedition landed on an island not far from High Rock. They too killed far more walruses than they could carry, and again the polar bears arrived to feast. More than 50 bears travelled to the island to dine. Unfortunately for many of them, hunters were waiting. They killed more than 20 of the bears, the rest escaping to the sanctuary of the sea ice.

·Leigh Smith and his high-born friend Lord David Kennedy had hunted polar bears on Spitsbergen in 1859. They pursued a sow and two cubs. The bears were on land, much of it mud. The hunters, who were in a boat parallel to the bears, fired a shot that hit the sow in the spine, paralyzing her immediately. With that potential menace incapacitated, the men overpowered the cubs. Leigh Smith was startled to find that when he slit open the bear's stomach, preparatory to skinning her, the orphans set to work cannibalizing their mother. The two cubs were eventually sold to a Paris zoo, only to become victims of the Franco-Prussian War. During the siege of Paris between September 1870 and the end of January 1871, the hungry citizens invaded the zoo and butchered the inhabitants, including the polar bears, for their own survival.

Later in 1871, Leigh Smith bemoaned the scarcity of game in one familiar cove on Spitsbergen, complaining, "Since I had hunted this bay—every spot of which I remembered so well—ten years exactly had gone by . . . and what had I seen since to equal the sport which had marked every creek and shallow and rock with the red cross of a kill." Leigh Smith continued his complaint, "But, alas, there is no longer occupation for a gentleman sportsman; the country is quite hunted out; there are no longer walruses, bears, or even seals." Leigh Smith was talking about the year 1871, but 130 years later, the Arctic is still suffering from the effects of overhunting.

When members of a 1931 expedition to Greenland allowed a polar bear and her cub to escape without shooting them, they were told by the captain of their ship that "allowing two bears to get off scot-free was not in accordance with Arctic traditions." It is a telling and depressing statement that does much to explain the attitude of explorers from a few generations back.

Newfoundlander Robert Bartlett, considered to be the foremost ice navigator of his time, led many expeditions into the Arctic. Some were for discovery, some for science, and at least one was for his clients' pure love of killing. In 1910, while on a European lecture tour, Captain Bartlett was contacted by American millionaire playboys Harry Whitney and Paul Rainey. What they wanted was simple, at least to them: a shooting expedition in the Arctic, and they were prepared to spend $100,000 to make it happen.

Bartlett raced back to North America and put the expedition together as fast as possible. Based on a 470-ton steel-hulled icebreaker named *Beothic*, the shooting party would go to Greenland, Baffin Island and deeper into the North. Their targets would be muskox, walrus and polar bears—as many as they could possibly bag in the short Arctic season.

By the time the ship turned for home, the bloodthirsty

This magnificent polar bear prowls in search of seals on an ice floe in Hudson Bay near Cape Churchill, Manitoba. ANSGER WALK

riflemen had killed 59 polar bears and an uncounted number of muskox and walrus. One report said they wiped out a herd of 24 muskox on Devon Island alone. They also brought back one adult bear and two cubs, two baby walrus and six muskox calves, all to be sold to American zoos. The adult bear was later named Silver King. He was a six-year-old that Bartlett captured in Jones Sound and was said to be the first adult male polar bear to be taken alive anywhere in the Arctic. Silver King was lassoed by Bartlett from a small boat and shipped to the Bronx Zoo, where he lived until his death in 1931.

Three years after the extravagant and extensive wildlife plunder of the Whitney-Rainey expedition, Bartlett was in the western Arctic as captain of the ill-fated *Karluk*. Bartlett was up in the crow's nest, searching for a way through the ice off Alaska's north coast, when he saw a magnificent polar bear on the ice about 500 yards away. With him was a scientist, Bjarne Mamen. The two men watched the creature for a while, then Mamen returned to the deck, took a rifle and aimed at the bear. Bartlett called to him to shoot it. Mamen was too excited and missed with the first two shots. The third hit the bear and knocked it over, but it recovered and lumbered away before it could be hit again. As it was impossible to follow it, no one knows whether the wound was life-threatening or not. Probably no one really cared. To them it was just a bear, and there were sure to be more in the next few weeks. Less than an hour later, they saw a second bear, and a group of men on the ship aimed their rifles and fired away, but without doing the bear any damage. Bartlett took care of that. He stood in the bow and fired twice, hitting the bear both times and killing it. The bear was skinned and its pelt used for clothing; the meat was fed to the sled dogs on board.

On a subsequent expedition in 1926, Bartlett came upon a sow with two cubs. Probably deeming the sow too big to handle, he shot her and captured the cubs for the New York

Zoological Society. Not all of the expedition's polar bear hunts went as smoothly. In Foxe Channel in 1927, Bartlett's crew saw two full-grown bears. They shot one and lassoed the other. It was hauled on board, creating a certain amount of panic among the crew, especially when the bear broke free and suddenly had the run of the deck. It was empty anyway, except for the mate. All other crew members were climbing as high in the rigging as possible to avoid the furious beast. The mate ran below for a rifle and shot the bear before it could wreck the ship.

With the advent of aircraft and powerboats, later trophy hunters roamed the Arctic with high-powered rifles and shot bears from speeding boats and highly manoeuvrable low-flying helicopters. Those hunters, like Whitney and Rainey before them, killed countless numbers of polar bears in the name of sport. It is not unlikely that the current plight of these creatures has much to do with such barbarous acts.

In May 1910, the Icelandic-Canadian Vilhjalmur Stefansson hunted a polar bear on sea ice just off the Canadian mainland in Amundsen Gulf. What Stefansson did not know was that the bear was hunting him at the same time. The man was out hunting for meat; the bear was doing exactly the same. The two played out their similar roles as they had both learned from experience. The bear followed its well-honed instincts: the tried-and-true stalking procedures of its kind. Stefansson, however, had an unfair advantage—he carried a rifle.

The bear was sleeping on the ice and was first seen as a yellow blob against stark white. Stefansson watched it for a few minutes, seeing it wake up and stand for a moment to stretch. It then settled down again. Stefansson noted those movements and moved quickly to cover the few hundred yards that separated him from the bear, concerned that it might wake up again and move off unseen in any direction. The bear, in its turn, had either scented or seen the hunter. Using all its skills, it circled around behind Stefansson and followed the trail his human smell left in his wake.

When Stefansson reached the place where he had seen the bear, it was barren. There was no sign of the creature. He climbed a pressure ridge and scanned the area through his binoculars without success. Planning to try and pick up the bear's tracks on the ice, he started to climb down. Before he had covered more than a step or two, he heard a distinct hiss coming from above and behind him. Looking up, not 20 feet away, was the bear. Had the bear remained silent, it could have crossed the narrow gap between them in a single leap. Instead, it paid the ultimate penalty for one slight, unnecessary sound.

British explorer Gino Watkins, who died far too young at 25 years old in a kayaking accident off east Greenland, wrote of his first experience with polar bears. While sailing from Norway to Spitsbergen in 1927 for an expedition to explore Edgeøya, Watkins and his team saw two bears swimming among the ice floes ahead of the bows of the ship. One of the team members shot one bear as it clambered out onto an ice floe. Gino had a boat lowered and gave chase after the second animal. He shot it in the head, and they managed to recover both bears and skin them for their pelts.

On a later expedition in east Greenland, they had a similar occurrence, but were in a small boat. They saw a polar bear and chased it to get close-up photographs. According to Watkins, the bear cooperated: "He got on to a floe and posed very nicely." On expeditions, one has to be prepared for emergencies at any time and without warning. The photographers found this out. "Then, at the critical moment, something went wrong with the engine. The boat ran at full speed head-on to the floe on which the bear was standing. [Spencer] Chapman who was in the bows managed somehow to keep his feet and his head. He threw down the camera and picked up his rifle, and, poking it in the bear's face, shot him stone dead just as he was about to jump into the boat."

After Gino Watkins' tragic death, his team members continued with the year-long Greenland expedition. Six months into their work, Spencer Chapman was hunting with three Inuk when they saw a bear following the tracks of their sled. They were out on the broken ice of a fjord at the time. On this occasion, the bear was needed for its meat, so some of the dogs were released to chase it while the sled followed. That bear did its utmost to outwit its pursuers. Chapman explained, "When we caught up we found that the bear had slipped down into the tide-crack, and with only his head showing was growling defiance at the dogs who barked excitedly only a yard or two away. When the dogs got too near, the bear would make sudden lunges at them, coming half out of the water. Sometimes he would dive, rarely staying under water for more than half a minute, to appear again further along the tide-crack."

One of the Inuk was able to harpoon the bear to prevent it diving again and then shot it in the neck. Although the meat was needed, and he had been an active participant in a few bear hunts, Chapman found the modern methods of simply shooting bears from a distance less than palatable. He commented, "In the old days when [the Inuit] killed bears with lances (as they still do from kayaks) bear hunting must have been quite exciting. But this is just butchery."

In the 1930s, Constable Jack Doyle of the RCMP was based at Pond Inlet, on the northern extremity of Baffin Island, for several years. The territory he patrolled was vast, taking him as far south as Igloolik on Fury and Hecla Strait and as far west as Somerset Island. Doyle and his Inuit travelling companions regularly shot polar bears to feed their dogs. At Fury Point on Somerset Island, they killed seven polar bears in a short space of time for that purpose. One can only assume they had a heck of a lot of dogs with them to need so much meat.

Arctic and subarctic whalers were never slow in harvesting other creatures if there was a possibility of profit. Hundreds of walrus and various species of seals were taken by individual ships, as were any other creatures whose pelts had any value, including foxes, caribou and, of course, polar bears.

Scottish captain Osbert Forsyth-Grant, owner of the small whaling ketch *Snowdrop* and later the much larger topsail schooner *Seduisante*, took his ships from Dundee to the eastern Canadian Arctic on annual voyages between 1904 and 1911. In 1907, after hunting between Greenland's west coast and the east coast of Baffin Island, *Snowdrop's* crew had not caught a whale, but their tally was still high. They had taken 184 walrus, 190 seals, 50 foxes, 170 caribou, 10½ tons of unspecified oil—almost certainly from the walrus and seals—and 23 polar bears. The latter pelts were sold and often used to decorate mansions in Scotland.

One of the 23 bears taken was a live cub. According to Forsyth-Grant's biographers, *Snowdrop's* crew had to exercise the cub on the return voyage by attaching it to a long chain and letting it swim beside the ship occasionally while on the North Atlantic Ocean. Well-fed polar bear cubs grow quickly, however, and this one was no exception. It stretched in all directions and put on weight as the voyage progressed, getting stronger and stronger. The bear became a real challenge for the sailors assigned to look after it, and they were all happy to see it gone when they reached port. It is believed to have been sold to a British zoo after it arrived in Dundee.

After *Snowdrop* was wrecked in 1908, Forsyth-Grant purchased *Seduisante* and took her to the whaling grounds in 1910. At the end of that voyage, he had taken another 17 polar bears, in addition to a large number of other creatures. Forsyth-Grant, who was young and adventurous, stayed on in Greenland for the winter of 1910 to 1911, living with the Inuit, although he sent *Seduisante* home to Scotland with the cargo. When the ship returned to the Greenland coast in May 1911, Forsyth-Grant was ready to go hunting again, planning to collect the usual hundreds of walrus and seals and any polar bears that happened along. Even though he had been shipwrecked before, neither he nor his crew could have imagined the tragedy that was to follow.

Instead of sticking to his regular hunting grounds in Davis Strait, Forsyth-Grant is believed to have gone farther south and west through Hudson Strait and into Hudson Bay. There followed tales of mutiny and murder, none of which have been substantiated. What is known is that *Seduisante* was wrecked in a storm off Nottingham Island, and most of her crew died, including 31-year-old Forsyth-Grant. His body was never recovered for burial. All the walrus, blubber and polar bear pelts they had taken went to the bottom of Hudson Bay with the ship.

Other whalers had been taking polar bears wherever they found them for decades. A Dundee whaler named *Arctic* took 12 in 1873. How many the rest of the fleet took each summer during the long era of whaling in Canada's eastern Arctic, Hudson Strait and Hudson Bay is unknown, but the total must have been in the thousands.

5

Far North with an Intrepid Few

ENGLISH EXPLORER MARTIN LINDSAY, who was a member of Gino Watkins' British Arctic Air Route Expedition of 1930–31, wrote, "Polar exploration is not a science. Rather it is something between an art and a sport. So we find that it is the sport and the quest of adventure that send men to the polar regions."

It is true that many who ventured into the Arctic regions did so for the sport and for the glory. One in particular, however, went north for scientific reasons, as well as for the adventure.

The great Norwegian explorer Fridjtof Nansen and a crew of 12 men took the 128-foot-long *Fram* into the Arctic ice north of Siberia in the summer of 1893. Nansen's goal was to reach the farthest north ever attained by a ship—as far as the pole itself, he hoped. For three years, the purpose-built *Fram* drifted in the polar ice with her crew on board. Being in the Arctic and surrounded by ice for so many months, the Norwegian scientists and explorers had plenty of time to study the wildlife and found themselves being studied in return. Polar bears, ever inquisitive, especially when smells of food are in the air, often wandered up to the ship with sometimes frightening results.

Nansen's journals of the long, experimental voyage are filled with lively tales of encounters with polar bears on the ice. Although the expedition team, including Nansen, shot animals in self-defence and for food for themselves and the sled dogs, they also killed indiscriminately on many occasions.

Arctic foxes do not make good eating, yet the men on *Fram* shot them anyway, perhaps just because they were there. They did the same with walruses and with reindeer, on one occasion shooting far more than they could possibly use for food. On the same day, they killed two polar bears, neither of which had threatened the men in any way. But perhaps, in some ways, the killing of polar bears was justified. The bears were often a problem during the three years the ship spent in the icy regions. They visited the ship on many occasions, almost certainly drawn to it by the smells of cooking. On the occasions that bears came too close, even getting on board ship at times, the potential loss of human life was considerable, and they certainly lost dogs to bear attacks while the canines were chained up on deck. And yet, when it suited Nansen, he left the odd bear to live when he could have killed it cleanly and without risk to himself.

On October 2, 1893, three members of Nansen's team were collecting scientific data at the observatory tent a short distance from the ship. Looking up, one of them saw a bear nosing around the bow. Henrik Blessing elected to make his way as quietly as possible to the ship and warn the rest of the crew. The bear saw him immediately and turned in his direction. Blessing ran back to his companions, closely followed by the bear. Sigurd Hansen tried to make himself look as big as possible and yelled loudly, hoping to scare off the bear. Blessing and Hjalmar Johansen added their voices to Hansen's. Unfazed by the racket, the bear kept coming.

Hansen and Johansen armed themselves, ready for a spirited defence. Hansen picked up an ice staff, Johansen an axe. Blessing stood there empty-handed. As one, they launched themselves toward safety. Screaming at the top of their lungs that there was a bear, they ran for the ship while the bear investigated the tent.

Nansen heard the shouts, grabbed a rifle and ran on deck. The bear, which must have been very close, saw Nansen and stopped long enough for the expedition leader to shoot it in the neck. It dropped to the snow, and the panic was over.

Hansen and Johansen had another bear scare a week or so later. A bear had been shot beside *Fram* that morning.

Perhaps that lulled the men into a false sense of security. Hansen and Johansen were taking magnetic observations south of the ship. Nansen was on the ice studying a pool where new ice was forming. Peter Henriksen was on deck when he noticed another bear ambling straight for the ship. The bear saw Hansen and Johansen and changed direction, heading straight for them. Nansen, absorbed in his study of the pool, was unaware of anything wrong. Henriksen raised his rifle and pulled the trigger. The rifle misfired several times in quick succession before it finally went off. The ball hit the bear in the back and sheared through its chest. The impact was such that the bear reared up in pain, its forepaws clawing at the sky, then fell over. Hansen raced up and shot it twice more with his revolver.

In December of that year, another bear got on board in the night and attacked the dogs, killing three of them. The following morning, it almost got one of the men too. Hours after the bear took the dogs, the others were still barking. Henriksen went to check on the dogs but failed to take a gun with him. When he stepped off the ship, a bear went for him and bit him in the side. He was able to break free and scream for help as he climbed back on board, but he was a lucky man. The bear left him and pounced on one of the dogs, perhaps selecting it as easier prey. The situation then descended into near farce. Four men had rifles, none of which was loaded. While one scrambled for fresh cartridges, the others reached for any weapon available. At that time, the bear was close enough for a man to reach over the side of the ship and touch it. In the end, Johansen came up with a loaded rifle; he shot the bear but failed to kill it.

Furious, the bear released the dog and growled up at the men. Johansen fired again and again. The captive dog managed to get free and ran for its life, while the other dogs danced around the bear barking loudly. Nansen finished the bear off with a well-placed bullet to the head. When they examined it, they found a thin one-year-old. It was obviously starving, which was why it had been so determined to get at the dogs.

Nansen and his team killed mostly for food, but despite being men of science, they still often killed for the sheer thrill of it. As *Fram* closed with an ice floe, the men could see a fox ahead. Many would have been pleased just to watch the enticing creature. Not so a senior member of the crew. Nansen reported, "[The fox was] jumping backward and forward on the ice, taking the most wonderful leaps and enjoying life. Sverdrup sent a ball from the forecastle which put an end to it on the spot." Otto Sverdrup was the ship's captain. Soon afterward, two bears were seen on land. Nansen wrote, "But they disappeared before we got in to shoot them."

Nansen wrote of another occasion when an encounter with bears turned ugly, but for the bears instead of the men. Three bears, a mother and two half-grown cubs, got in among the dogs one night. Expedition members fired nine shots and heard one of the bears roaring horribly, as if in pain. Convinced it was badly wounded, they set off to finish the job. They found a dead cub with two holes in it, plus the tracks of two more bears. After skinning the dead bear, they returned to the ship, but Nansen went in pursuit of the other two the next day with some dogs. He found bloody tracks and the place where the crippled cub had spent the night. Close by were tracks of a larger bear, no doubt the mother.

Loping along on snowshoes, Nansen caught up with the injured cub as it tried to keep moving. The bear had been shot through the back, probably in the spinal area, and was dragging its hind legs across the ice. Seeing the pursuers, it took refuge in a hole in the ice and bobbed up and down in the water, constantly diving and returning for breath. Nansen said the dogs raced wildly around the hole, barking at the bear. He managed to slip a rope noose over one of the cub's paws and was then able to put it out of its misery. Although he and one of his men tracked the mother, they were unable to catch her. The incident had cost them two dogs, which at first Nansen thought might have been killed, although no trace of them was found. Alternatively, he guessed, they had run away in fright. One day later, the missing dogs returned to the ship.

Other dogs were killed by bears. On one occasion when a bear got aboard *Fram*, it managed to take two dogs, both of which it killed and partly ate out on the ice before getting away.

The scars on this bear's muzzle are from a fight with another bear.
ANTHONY DALTON

Otto Sverdrup built a complicated bear trap, but it was not successful. The first bear that came along studied it from all angles. Ignoring the fresh bait inside, it obviously sensed something was amiss and wisely left the trap alone. Then it made the mistake of heading straight for the ship and suffered a quick death.

Sometimes the ship and its crew were spared the attentions of bears for as long as three months. Then, for no apparent reason, they would come back. One day, after a long hiatus, four bears came close without causing harm and left without injury to themselves. They were among the lucky ones.

Peter Freuchen, the self-styled "Vagrant Viking" from Denmark, spent many years in the Arctic. While a member of Knud Rasmussen's Second Thule Expedition, from 1916 to 1918, he told of a somewhat farcical event concerning a polar bear in Greenland.

Freuchen, plus his Inuit wife, Navarana, and young son, Mequsaq, holed up in a cave with another Scandinavian and an Inuit companion to wait out a storm. As was customary, they tied the dogs outside but dragged the loaded sled into the cave with them. Freuchen's son woke in the night to see a polar bear on the sled. He told his mother, and she woke Freuchen. It was his habit to sleep naked in the fur sleeping bags. He could see the bear eating his walrus meat, but his rifle was on the sled.

Freuchen leapt out of his bag into the frigid air of -30°C and tried to get his pants on. In his haste, he said he put both legs down the same side of his pants and rolled across the floor of the cave, still mostly naked, and ended up very close to the bear. That creature, unimpressed by the sight, tried to escape, but the dogs had awakened at the noise. They ripped off their harnesses and raced into the cave. Freuchen described the chaotic scene, "The bear, Koch, Ituksuk, and I, not to mention thirty-eight dogs, were all running around in circles. The only one who enjoyed it was little Mequsaq, who screamed with laughter."

Two of the dogs were killed before someone was able to shoot the bear. It wasn't until the mayhem ceased that Freuchen and the other two men realized how exposed and terribly cold they were. At least they and the dogs had bear meat to sustain them for a few days afterward.

Another Scandinavian, the famed Norwegian explorer Roald Amundsen, almost lost his life to a polar bear on the Siberian coast in 1918. Amundsen had broken his shoulder in a fall on the ice and had one arm supported in a sling. He was out on the ice near the ship without a rifle, but with Jacob, one of his dogs. Jacob went off by himself but soon came racing back in alarm, chased by a polar bear. Amundsen made a run for the ship with Jacob, but the bear was too fast. The explorer and the bear reached the gangway together, and Amundsen was laid flat with a vicious blow to his back. He landed on his injured shoulder and was at the mercy of the bear until Jacob came to the rescue. The dog lured the bear away, and Amundsen lived to continue exploring.

When Canadian naturalist J. Dewey Soper went on his first Arctic expedition in 1923, part of his brief was to collect specimens of Canada's Arctic wildlife for the National Museum of Canada. That included polar bears. Soper saw his first polar bear from the foredeck of the CGS *Arctic* while the ship navigated through the ice between Greenland and Ellesmere Island in the extreme northern reaches of Baffin Bay. He shot that bear and preserved its pelt for eventual delivery to the museum. Later on the same expedition,

Soper counted six polar bears hunting seals together from ice in Lancaster Sound, but he left them alone. Additional sightings convinced him that, at that time, Lancaster Sound was home to a large number of bears.

On a subsequent two-year sojourn on Baffin Island, Soper was in a boat cruising up a fjord off Cumberland Sound when the boatman saw a polar bear swimming ahead of them. Although Soper shot the bear and collected its pelt, he was unhappy with the event. Shooting a swimming polar bear from a boat was, to him, rather like "shooting down a cow in a barnyard."

In the mid-1950s, a young Scotsman named Duncan Pryde joined the Hudson's Bay Company and went to work in the Arctic. In his autobiography, *Nunaga: Ten Years of Eskimo Life*, Pryde wrote of the times he crossed paths with polar bears. He admitted, without showing any remorse, that he had killed or helped kill bears. The first such occasion was in winter, while travelling between Spence Bay and Gjoa Haven with an Inuit companion.

The dogs found the den of a female with two cubs. The men broke open the snow den, shot the sow and then shot the two cubs because they would be too much trouble to keep. Although he did not say so, it is assumed that Pryde and his partner skinned the bears to sell the pelts and kept the meat for their dog team.

From his base on Perry Island, on the south shore of Queen Maud Gulf, Pryde went on an extended polar bear hunt for about a month with four local Inuit. They spent the first 10 days travelling over land and sea ice to reach the north coast of Victoria Island. There they came across a scattered grouping of bears. Wending their sleds through the jumbled ice along shore, the men had to be careful that no bears followed with a view to setting up an ambush.

Moving far out on the sea ice of Viscount Melville Sound, Pryde and his Inuit hunting partner Nasarlulik tracked one bear that was working its way from one seal breathing hole to the next. They soon saw it waiting at a hole for a seal. The dog teams sensed or smelled the bear and started barking as they raced across the ice pulling the sled, which was empty except for the two men.

The bear heard the dogs when they were still a few hundred yards away, and it took off. As was customary, Pryde released some of the team to chase the bear, while the men followed with the sled and the remaining animals. When the loose dogs caught up with the bear and surrounded it, the bear swiped one big paw at a dog that came too close and threw it high into the air, killing it instantly. When Pryde arrived, he stood clear of the melee and shot the bear in the head.

The other three hunters returned later with seven more bears between them. That haul guaranteed there was enough meat for dog feed so they could stay on the site for at least a week. A few days after the first kills, Pryde and Nasarlulik came upon two sows with two cubs apiece. Seeing the men and hearing the dogs, the adult bears charged to protect their young. In the ensuing battle, both adult bears were shot, as was one of the cubs. Two more cubs fell to the hunters' bullets soon after, while the fourth young one escaped. During that month of killing, 5 men shot 26 polar bears.

During the British Trans-Arctic Expedition of 1968–69, four explorers crossed the Arctic on foot and with dog sleds from Point Barrow, Alaska, to Spitsbergen via the North Pole. Wally Herbert (later Sir Wally) was the leader. They had a few run-ins with polar bears, most of those in the latter stages of the expedition. Wally wrote of his appreciation for them and of the team's problems with polar bears as they approached the end of their long journey. "They are very fearsome, but very beautiful, too. When they are some distance off, they are magnificent beasts, but when they come closer and closer, they do become very menacing. They just amble toward you with a completely fearless expression on their faces . . . They don't look you straight in the eye and come toward you; they casually close the distance."

Herbert's team did their best to scare off all polar bears that came too close. When that proved fruitless, they opened fire, but always waited as long as possible before pulling their triggers. That meant if the bear or bears came closer than 20 feet, they would shoot. Even that was cutting it fine: a polar bear can cross a distance of 20 feet in seconds. On the occasions when they were forced to kill a bear, they carved up the carcass and fed the meat to the dogs. That, inevitably, created a new problem. The dogs associated polar bears with fresh meat. Whenever a bear came in sight, the dogs became almost uncontrollable.

Just north of Phipps Island, on the northern perimeter of the Spitsbergen group, Herbert's team had to keep a constant watch. "Polar bear tracks . . . were all over the place. There were literally hundreds and hundreds of tracks going in every direction." On the last few days of the crossing, where the ice was broken up and getting mushy, the expedition members were regularly stalked by at least one and sometimes two bears. At that time, they were running out of ammunition, and killing a determined polar bear, they found, usually entailed three or four shots, which they could not afford. Herbert noted that they threw ice axes at one bear, without stopping its advance, and his spare boots at another. That bear tore the boots to pieces. Nothing seemed to deter them, except bullets.

Despite their lack of ammunition and the constant aggressive approaches by polar bears, the 4 men and 34 huskies of the British Trans-Arctic Expedition kept moving across the ice until they were picked up by a Royal Navy ship just off the coast of Spitsbergen. The resident polar bears went back to hunting seals.

6

Tales from Churchill and Hudson Bay

CHURCHILL, MANITOBA, ON THE WESTERN shore of Hudson Bay, is known as the Polar Bear Capital of the World. It is a grand title for marketing purposes, and there is much substance to the claim. Polar bears have made Churchill famous. Despite its apparent isolation, Churchill is easily reached by air or train from Winnipeg. It has an excellent and well-established tourism infrastructure that caters efficiently to visitors, especially the hordes of polar bear watchers who arrive in the fall.

Churchill is a seaport town of approximately 1,000 human residents and an ever-changing population of polar bears in the surrounding area. The bears are most visible in October and November. At that time of the year, they relocate from the tundra, their summer habitat, and congregate along the shores of Hudson Bay, waiting for the sea ice to form. They also are known to wander through Churchill, savouring the smells and taking snacks at the garbage dump on the town's outskirts.

While the bears wait for winter to build the ice on the bay, tourists arrive in their hundreds to see polar bears close up and personal. Elaborate and rather ungainly-looking vehicles known as Tundra Buggies take tourists out onto the snow-covered land and along the shores to meet polar bears face to face. The vehicles have huge tires, specifically · designed to minimize their impact on the tundra. They also serve to elevate the passenger compartments on the enormous buggies so that bears can look up at the big windows and see the passengers but cannot climb aboard.

Tundra Buggy drivers are adept at finding the bears, and if none are at first visible, they have ways to attract them. Understanding the bears' acute sense of smell, the drivers often open a small tin of sardines and let the fishy aromas drift on the breeze. The polar bears soon come in search of the source of the enticement. Once the ice is frozen hard, however, usually in early November, the bears move offshore to hunt seals, and the Tundra Buggies are returned to storage for another year. That doesn't mean all the bears have gone, as some come back at odd times. For this reason, Parks Canada rangers maintain a year-round polar bear watch, as do all the residents.

Len Smith, the designer of the Tundra Buggy, shows off two of his early giant vehicles in Churchill, Manitoba. ANTHONY DALTON

The two Churchill deaths related to polar bears took place in 1968 and 1983. In the first incident, a group of local teenagers found polar bear tracks in soft snow and followed them through the town. When they caught up with the bear, they foolishly antagonized it by throwing rocks at it. The bear—no surprise here—got mad and attacked them, killing one boy. Local authorities shot the bear.

In the second instance, a man took advantage of the fire that destroyed the Churchill Hotel, scavenging through the ruins. He found a freezer of meat and helped himself to a few choice cuts, stuffing them into his pockets. Unfortunately for him, a polar bear was within sniffing range and soon followed its nose to the delightful smell of fresh meat. In the ensuing disagreement about ownership of the loot, the bear killed the man and took the meat. That bear too was subsequently shot. One hopes it had time to eat its hard-won meal before it died.

Long before modern conservation efforts, polar bears found wandering through Churchill were shot as menaces and their meat used to feed sled dogs. During the Second World War, when there was a military air base near Churchill, American and other servicemen shot bears for sport and shipped the pelts home as trophies. Today, with tourism a major money-maker for Churchill residents, polar bears are protected and considered an asset to the community.

There are some wonderful anecdotes about encounters with Churchill's bears published on Internet websites. Of those, the following tales are guaranteed to amuse.

When a bear ambled into the Royal Canadian Legion hall looking for something to eat, the club steward shouted at it, "You're not a member! Get out!" The bear obeyed and left the premises immediately.

A local family made the mistake of leaving leftover chicken in their kitchen, where it could be smelled by active noses. They went off to attend a school concert. While they were enjoying the entertainment, a bear wandering in the neighbourhood broke in and ate the chicken. It sensibly left before the family returned and so lived to forage another day.

As proof that size does not always matter, a tiny but courageous Churchill woman refused to be intimidated by a polar bear nosing about on her porch. She fetched her broom and chased the bear away by whacking its bottom with the bristly sweeper. Another local—a trapper—was heating up some fish stew when a bear happened by and decided to join in the meal. The trapper got rid of the bear by banging two metal pie plates together.

One polar bear became confused by too many good smells. It approached the town's Harbour Board kitchen in search of the source of several enticing odours. Finding and carrying away a bag of smelly garbage, the bear's nose let it down somewhat. Had it taken the time to look around, it would have seen a pile of tasty pork chops resting on the counter.

In 1982, concerned about the number of bears found wandering about town and rummaging through the local dump, the town authorities built a polar bear jail nearby. Nuisance bears are tranquilized, collected in handy escape-proof trailers and incarcerated in the jail until it's time to ship them out. The sedated miscreants then take a helicopter ride, slung under the aircraft in a strong net, for a couple of hundred miles to the north and are set free. Some determined individuals find their way back in just a few days.

Polar bear traps are lined up outside the polar bear jail in Churchill, Manitoba. ANTHONY DALTON

Although it hasn't eliminated the problem of polar bear–human confrontations, Churchill's purpose-built jail has certainly reduced the threat.

Known as the "Eagle," Steve Miller is a Churchill-based helicopter pilot who probably knows more about the polar bears of the west side of Hudson Bay than anyone else. He has met most of them. Far more than 5,000 bears have been subjected to Steve's close scrutiny, and a large percentage of those have flown with him from Churchill to more remote locations. When scientists need to locate and examine a bear, they contact Steve Miller to fly them in.

An October 1999 television news report stated, "Eighty percent of the adult [polar] bears in the Churchill area have been tranquillized, handled, tagged, tattooed, weighed and measured, had blood drawn, teeth checked, their behaviour and life history recorded, more than once." It is an impressive declaration, and Steve Miller almost certainly was involved in some way with every one of those contacts.

In the summer of 1993, I flew with Steve in his helicopter far and wide across the tundra surrounding Churchill. He told me then, as we hovered over the concentrated jagged floes of sea ice looking for bears, "I guess I've handled more polar bears than any other pilot." At that time, he recounted with a smile, he had handled 2,698 in the previous 10 years.

Talking about nuisance bears, Steve said that it takes less than two minutes from the time the bear is drugged by a dart fired from a special rifle until it falls, unharmed but very sleepy. The bear is checked and tagged where it falls. "Checking" means examining teeth and gums, taking blood samples, looking for signs of disease and injury, and more, before the bear is taken aloft in a net slung under the helicopter and removed from the area.

Each morning at Cape Merry in Churchill, where the Churchill River flows into Hudson Bay, local rangers begin their day with a polar bear watch, scanning the slowly drifting ice and the shoreline for any signs of the predators. Most days in summer, all they see are beluga whales cruising past, moving in and out of the estuary. But occasionally they discover a bear and have to persuade it to stay away from town.

The wreck of an old freighter, the SS *Ithaca*, sits upright on the mud flats in Bird Cove, just to the east of Churchill. It has been there for decades after running aground in a storm in 1961. The local polar bears are often to be seen on the mud flats and boulder-strewn seabed at low tide around the ship, between July and the beginning of the ice in late October and early November.

Fears of polar bears around the extensive shores of Hudson Bay are well founded. Canoeists completing their journeys down the rapids of the Hayes or Seal rivers, both of which empty into Hudson Bay, are always on the lookout for bears as they approach the coast. And they should be. The old Hudson's Bay Company post at York Factory on the Hayes River and the Seal River Heritage Lodge north of Churchill are regularly visited by polar bears, and with no medical facilities for long distances, extreme caution is required.

In July 1999, an undernourished juvenile bear, no more than 1½ years old and weighing about 250 pounds, went on a rampage at Corbett Inlet, 30 miles south of Rankin Inlet, on the west side of Hudson Bay. By the time it was over, one woman was dead and two other people were recovering from their injuries.

On that sad occasion, a group of five Natives were camped in tents near the Hudson Bay shore. Earlier that day, their boat had drifted away, and they were understandably concerned about it. One man, Moses Aliyak, and his

12-year-old grandson, Cyrus, decided to go looking for it. Also at the camp were 64-year-old Hattie Amitnak, her 56-year-old stepdaughter, Margaret Amarook, and 10-year-old Eddie Amitnak, Hattie's grandson.

Margaret had gone alone to a spring to collect fresh water when Moses and Cyrus left their tent and walked in the direction where the boat had last been seen. Unknown to them, a polar bear watched them leave from close to their tent. Margaret had expected others to help her with the water, knowing it would be heavy. When no one showed up, she began to be concerned and returned to the camp carrying one heavy pail of water.

While Margaret was gone from the camp, the bear had attacked Moses as he and Cyrus set off for the boat. Moses fought back, throwing stones at the bear and shouting. The bear was not deterred, and his claws sliced into Moses' head and face, cutting him badly. Cyrus, meanwhile, ran back to the tent in fear. Hattie and Eddie ran to help Moses, but the little boy took a smack from a big paw and suffered head injuries. Hattie went for the bear without a weapon and was quickly overwhelmed. The bear mauled her to death.

Margaret was walking back into camp with her head down, carrying the water container, when she glanced up and saw a polar bear eating something beside her tent. The bear looked right at her. None of the others were in sight. Then she heard Moses calling to her. "He said come. So I went to him," Margaret said.

Moses was hiding in the remains of an old cabin. When Margaret found him, he was unrecognizable, with blood all over his head. He told her to go far away from the campsite. From the tent, Cyrus also called out to warn her there was a polar bear nearby and to stay away.

Margaret, of course, was worried about the injuries Moses had suffered, but he convinced her he would stay in the wrecked cabin and would be okay. At that point, Margaret ran for the camp of friends, nearly two miles away. When she looked back, she saw that Moses had changed his mind and was following her, despite his injuries. She chose to keep running, knowing that her friends, David and Rosie Oolooyuk, had a single-sideband radio that she could use to get help.

Before long, two helicopters came over the horizon, the chopping of their rotors giving immediate comfort to Margaret. On board were RCMP officers, two trauma nurses and wildlife officers. The three injured people were taken away immediately to be airlifted to a hospital in Winnipeg. It was too late for Hattie Amitnak; she was already dead. Meanwhile, the wildlife officers soon found the bear nearby, killed it cleanly and sent the body to be studied under autopsy in Saskatoon in an attempt to determine why it attacked the people.

One of the wildlife officers commented that attacks on humans by polar bears are rare. "It's really uncommon," he said. "There's only been a few cases in the last twenty years."

7

Polar Bears
on Display

POLAR BEARS ARE NOT REALLY territorial. In the wild, they are used to roaming vast distances alone in search of food or a mate. Marking such enormous tracts of moving ice in order to claim it as their own would be an impossibility. Except in the loosest possible terms, polar bears do not normally stay in a self-designated area. They are the ultimate symbols of freedom on land or sea ice.

When taken out of their natural domain and exhibited in zoos, polar bears are immediately confined to a small enclosure, which is surrounded by a safety barrier of some kind. The bears can reach any corner of their prison within seconds. For a creature that habitually walks hundreds of miles each year, the sudden insurmountable boundaries create impossibly cramped conditions, no matter how well-designed the setting.

According to Polar Bears International, there are a minimum of 110 zoos in the world that house at least one polar bear. Some have two or three in residence.

Certainly the most famous zoo inmate, at least until her death in November 2008, was Winnipeg's Debbie. Born in Russia's far north in 1966 and orphaned soon after, Debbie spent her early months in a Dutch zoo before being shipped to Winnipeg's Assiniboine Park Zoo in 1967. She quickly became a star and was visited by an estimated 15 million people in her four decades at the zoo. Debbie was listed in the 2008 edition of the Guinness Book of World Records as the world's oldest living polar bear.

Debbie's mate, Skipper, lived a long life too. Between them, they had six offspring between 1974 and 1984. All the cubs were eventually sent to zoos in Germany, Ireland and Japan. Skipper was a Canadian, born on Baffin Island, and he died in the zoo in 1999, aged 34. In a rather considerate gesture, he was cremated and his ashes were taken back to the Arctic and scattered over the island of his birth.

Debbie lived to be 42, an impressive age considering that polar bears in the wild rarely survive longer than 20 years and usually considerably less. Despite her age, Debbie does not hold the record for polar bear longevity. That honour goes to Doris. She was born in the wild but spent most of her life in the Detroit Zoo, where she reached the grand old age of 43 years and 8 months. The vast difference between the life spans of captive bears and their wild relatives can be explained by the care and attention lavished on most bears in zoos. They tend to eat better and have access to excellent medical care.

Some captive bears, however, live out miserable lives in appalling conditions. American author David Roberts recalled a polar bear that he saw in the Denver Zoo when he was a boy. It was, he said, blind and toothless and paced a few paces one way and the same number back all day long in a compound too small for true exercise. That captive bear's pacing had worn a rut in the concrete floor. Many years later, in 1994, the Denver Zoo introduced Klondike and Snow to the public. In one year they grew to over 300 pounds apiece and were far too big for their unnatural city home. To give them more space, they were sent to Florida to SeaWorld of Orlando, where they joined the cast at Base Station Wild Arctic.

In some zoos, keepers become surrogate parents and, in many cases, friends to their charges. This is not always to the benefit of the animal, but exceptional examples of human and polar bear bonding have occasionally occurred. In those instances, a few interesting and harmless experiments have been conducted on polar bears in zoos, sometimes quite unexpectedly.

When she worked at the Detroit Zoo, biologist and bear expert Else Poulsen looked after a polar bear named Sissy, among other responsibilities. After a series of dental

Polar bears are powerful swimmers and can cover long distances in Arctic seas. This captive polar bear enjoys swimming in its large pool at the Louisville Zoo in Kentucky. L. SHEARS

operations, Sissy was not feeling well. Offering her a trickle of warm water to drink from a hose, Poulsen was surprised to see the bear soak her paw in the water and then wash her face. When she finished, she slapped her right leg, directing the zookeeper where to spray the water. Sissy then washed that leg. The exercise was repeated, with Sissy taking the initiative as she ordered Poulsen to wet her other legs and hip, and finally her head. After each body part had been soaked in turn, the bear washed herself thoroughly and soon showed signs of feeling much better. There was no doubt that Sissy was in charge of the ablutions, not her highly educated keeper.

Else Poulsen wrote of giving one polar bear a new lease on life. The bear had suffered abuse for far too many years in a circus—probably cooped up in a small cage as part of a menagerie. When Poulsen took over Bärle's welfare at the Detroit Zoo, she started by giving the sad bear a huge treat. Clean straw! Poulsen's description of the bear's joy at this unexpected gift shows what wonders love for another creature can achieve: "She flopped sideways into the pile [of clean straw] and rolled on her back, feet in the air, rubbing, gyrating, a smile on her face, saliva running from her nose and mouth. She seemed to be experiencing pure pleasure."

The Berlin Zoo in Germany experienced a huge rush of worldwide attention in March 2006, when the owners showed off Knut for the first time. Knut was born in the zoo but abandoned by his mother. For the first four months of

Knut, a popular resident of the Berlin Zoo, was depicted on a German postage stamp in 2008. DEUTSCHE POST AG

his life, he was bottle-fed by the polar bear keeper, Thomas Dörflein, who cared for him around the clock. Knut, who was also undeniably cute and photogenic, even for a baby bear, became a monumental media star. He was fortunate that the German environment minister, Sigmar Gabriel, had adopted him at birth and paid for his care. Of course, the good minister had an ulterior motive. In return for Gabriel's financial consideration, Knut became the logo for the German campaign against global warming and the official symbol of a conference for endangered species held in Berlin in 2008. It was a master stroke on Herr Gabriel's part. He singlehandedly raised awareness of polar bears and helped the cause of those studying and fighting climate change at the same time. As a result of the publicity and worldwide attention, Knut even earned the distinction of having his portrait featured on a German postage stamp.

Knut, of course, did not remain a cute, cuddly little white bear. He grew and grew over the first year until, at 300 pounds or more, he became a big, aggressive-looking inmate of the zoo, with often-dirty white fur. With the inevitable change in his appearance, his appeal to the masses lessened. He is now just a better–known-than-most polar bear in a zoo.

In the early part of the 20th century, large carnivores were the main features in extravagant circus acts. Despite their size and ability to kill prey—or a man—with a single blow, polar bears tend to look rather docile and, to an extent, quite cuddly. Those are not necessarily desirable attributes in the circus world, where much of the entertainment aims to titillate the audiences' senses with displays of flirtation with danger. That drawback notwithstanding, polar bears were used as circus acts and were somewhat successful.

Ringling Bros. and Barnum & Bailey's Circus featured groups of polar bears in action under the big top as recently as 1977. One of their advertising posters from that year shows nine polar bears doing various tricks, plus a roaring tiger. Earlier posters from the same circus showed polar bears roller skating hand in hand, riding bicycles, beating drums, climbing ladders and wrestling with their trainers.

A German entrepreneur, Carl Hagenbeck, collected

exotic wild creatures and sold them to zoos and circuses in the late 1800s and early 1900s. Hagenbeck also had his own travelling circus. At one time, the main attraction was a huge collection of 75 adult polar bears, each of which had been trained to perform by the owner's brother.

Another German, the diminutive Ursula Bottcher, made a big name for herself in Europe and America with her stable of 10 performing polar bears in a show billed as "Beauty and the Beasts." Any one of the bears could have turned on her at any time. She is reported to have said, "If I gave them the chance, they would eat me."

Polar bears in zoos have attacked patrons and, on a couple of occasions, tried to eat them. In each case, the fault was with a visitor or visitors climbing over the protecting rails, fences or walls to get close to the bears. The most recent was in Berlin in April 2009.

A 32-year-old woman wearing slacks and a dark T-shirt climbed over a retaining barrier and jumped into the polar bears' enclosure at feeding time. As she swam across a small moat, one of the four bears in the enclosure attacked her. Why? Possibly it thought she was there to play. Most probably, though, the bear reacted instinctively, seeing her as a large seal and therefore its favourite meal. The woman survived only because of the quick thinking of six zoo attendants. They hurled safety rings attached to ropes to distract the bears and lowered another rope to the woman. As she desperately tried to climb to safety, one of the bears repeatedly grabbed at her with its paws and bit her. She lost her grip on the rope during her first attempt to climb out and fell back into the pool, where the bears awaited. As she went underwater, one of the bears dived down toward her. Only the action of more life rings hitting the water diverted what would have been an inevitable and probably fatal attack. When she was finally dragged out of reach by rescuers, the woman had multiple injuries to her arms and legs. Although severely injured and needing surgery, the woman survived.

There are many similar stories of people not understanding the dangers in encroaching on the habitat of captive bears. In 1994, an Australian woman was attacked at the Alaska Zoo in Anchorage when she chose to ignore the safety barrier and climbed over it to get closer for a photograph. Binky, one of the resident polar bears, bit her on the leg.

Three preteen boys decided to cool off with a dip in the polar bear pool at Brooklyn's Prospect Park Zoo in the early summer of 1987. They broke into the zoo after hours and climbed "a high spiked fence" to access the bears' enclosure. One of the boys stripped off and plunged in. Two curious polar bears ambled down from their dens on the rocky mount enclosed by the moat and grabbed the boy. Whether it was their intention to play or to feed will never be known. Either way, the boy did not stand a chance and was quickly killed. When police arrived in response to an emergency call, about 20 minutes later, the bears were still mauling the obviously dead child. Four police officers blasted away at the bears with a shotgun and their revolvers until they fell.

Five years before, New York had experienced another fatality caused by illegal and irresponsible entry into a polar bear compound. On that occasion, a 29-year-old man climbed into the danger zone at Central Park Zoo and was killed by 1,200-pound Scandy.

Each of the above stories was widely reported, yet gruesome stories and graphic videos fail to deter everyone. Nothing, it seems, will stop a determined person from climbing obvious barriers to get too close to dangerous animals in zoos.

8

Modern Adventurers in the Northwest Passage

DESPITE THE FACT THAT so many early Arctic explorers died in the quest to find a way through the Northwest Passage, modern adventurers have continued to pit themselves against the unpredictable ice. Inevitably, while camped onshore or caught in the ice, they have been targeted by polar bears.

British adventurer and round-the-world sailor David Scott Cowper took a converted lifeboat through the Northwest Passage in the late 1980s. He had enough encounters with polar bears on that voyage to last him the rest of his life. On one occasion, he reported, "I was working on one of the propellers at low tide. I glanced up . . . to find a polar bear not 12 feet away. I am not sure which one of us had the biggest fright but at least he (or she) was surprised enough to stand still while I clambered rather smartly back on board."

Obviously intrigued by Cowper, the bear did not go away. Instead it decided to take a closer look. "After a while, the bear came right up to the boat and stood on its hind legs with front paws resting on the rubber fender and huge face peering through the lifelines. Thinking that this was quite close enough I shouted in what I hoped was a threatening manner bringing a snarl in reply. As its paws slipped down the fender, the claws gouged out marks that left no doubt as to their sharpness."

The bear did not go far. It wandered over to inspect Cowper's cans of diesel fuel, kit bags and then his dinghy. "I did not object to him sniffing at it, or even bouncing up and down on it but had to take exception when he started to bite the rubber." Cowper fired a warning shot, and the bear left the dinghy and wandered away. It did come back but never showed threatening behaviour.

The following year, while preparing to continue his expedition with his wife, Caroline, Cowper had another close call with a polar bear. The couple were camped in an abandoned Hudson's Bay Company hut, with the boat close by. Early in the morning, Cowper heard a loud rattling at the door. "There was a thud. Up at the window in the door were two huge paws the size of dinner plates and a black nose while a pair of large black eyes peered in at us."

The bear went away but came back a few minutes later and looked in again. By this time, the Cowpers had retreated to a raised platform near the inside of the roof. From there, they could look out a small window and still see the bear, and it could see them. David Cowper wrote, "Neither of us will forget the stare he gave us: if looks could kill we would have been dead on the spot." The bear soon lost interest, and after destroying a few bags of provisions and a tarpaulin, it left the scene.

American sailor Alvah Simon and his wife, Diana, took his 36-foot white-hulled sailboat to the Arctic in June 1994, with the intention of spending months exploring the ice and the islands. When conditions deteriorated, they decided to winter over in a secluded bay on the west side of Bylot Island. There, as Simon was busy securing his craft and shutting down the engine, Diana told him to turn around. A lone wanderer was on the shore to greet them. Simon wrote, "A giant male polar bear stormed down the gravel beach, crashed through the ice and aimed straight for us."

The bear, a lean and hungry one, went to enormous lengths to disguise its approach and intentions. The two figures on the boat would have looked like seals to him. He wanted food, and it was right there in front of him. He went into hunting mode immediately.

Roger Henry, Simon's boat, was tucked up against a wall of ice that would give the bear a distinct advantage if it chose to take that route. Although the danger was acute, Alvah and

Diana were fascinated by the efforts the bear made to avoid being detected by his intended prey. The bear swam strongly but smoothly toward the boat, underwater some of the time, breaking through thin ice to breathe at others. When he was almost beside the boat, the bear surfaced, poking the top half of his head through the slush to look directly at Simon. Face to face but out of reach, the bear changed its tactics. Simon wrote, "He burst out of the water onto the tall pan [of ice], looming above us, fully exposed in awful dimension."

The sound of air horns unsettled the bear but did not scare it off. It stayed there, swaying, moving forward when all was quiet, lurching back each time the horn blared. Tiring of the noise, the bear slid back into the water. Behind the boat, it stopped and piled slushy ice on its head to change its profile. Then it waited. Simon watched and waited too. Each time the bear opened an eye, Simon yelled at it; finally the bear gave up and returned to shore. The first encounter had ended in a sort of win for the man.

Over the months that *Roger Henry* lay more or less entombed in ice, Simon had many encounters with bears. Some climbed on board to study the boat or to eat whatever appeared edible. Others came by but ignored the ice-encrusted vessel. When the ice broke up and Simon was working his boat through the ice floes of Navy Board Inlet, heading for Lancaster Sound, seeing polar bears close up became an accepted part of the scenery. One bear, swimming hard, actually passed the boat and kept on going.

A US Navy submarine surfacing through the north polar ice cap is a curiosity much too interesting for a trio of polar bears to ignore.
CHIEF YEOMAN ALPHONSO BRAGGS, US NAVY

Alvah Simon deliberately risked his life to challenge a polar bear on the shores of Lancaster Sound. The initial meeting was quite accidental. The bear wandered into view, but fortunately Simon was downwind, so the bear did not catch his scent. Simon, armed with a rifle, followed the bear for some distance, placing his feet in the bear's footprints. He was not intending to kill the creature, only examining his own courage and trying to be as strong as his Inuit friends. When he was close enough to smell the bear, Simon called out, and the bear turned to face him. The puny man and fully grown polar bear stared at each other. Simon laid his rifle on the snow and took a long stride forward, closer to the bear. He took another step. "The bear," Simon wrote, "grunted and rocked forward." The unarmed man held his hands up, palms facing the bear, and stood his ground as the bear moved closer. Towering over the man, the bear could have killed him with one casual blow from a front paw. Instead, it turned on its heels and ran away.

There are those who would say Alvah Simon was foolish. Many would say he was lucky to live through the faceoff. He saw it differently. Expressing a quasi-religious senti- ment, he accepted that the bear had handed him his life and had done so for a purpose far more complex than he, or we, could understand.

While paddling north in 1988 to make a crossing of Smith Sound, en route by kayak from Ellesmere Island to Greenland, Jon Turk and his wife, Chris, came face to face with a polar bear. They had been in close proximity to six bears a few days earlier in Makinson Inlet. On that occa- sion, the bears were all moving purposefully toward the east, though not together. First came "a mother with two cubs, then a lone male, then another female with one cub."

North and east of Makinson Inlet, Turk was climbing a rocky outcrop when he saw a large white creature above him. Turk went down a step or two to get out of reach of the bear's paws, while the bear peered over the rim of the rock. They stared at each other for what must have seemed like a lifetime to Turk, then the bear turned away and left him alone.

This time, out on the open sea ice, the bear was not much more than a few hundred yards away. It wasn't just ambling east like the other bears, going in the same direction as the Turks, it was coming straight at them—and at speed. While Jon was trying to ready his rifle, Chris ran at the bear, shouting loudly, and she blocked Jon's aim at the same time. They were both lucky. The bear slowed its charge, changed direction and took off through the broken and rafted ice.

The Turks had met a pair of archaeologists camped on the shores of Melville Island a few days before. They had told of the couple of bears harassing their camp, almost certainly attracted by the smell of food.

Manitoban adventurer Don Starkell is no stranger to paddling his kayak in extreme conditions. He had already paddled from Winnipeg to the Amazon when he began planning a similar voyage through the Northwest Passage. For Starkell, however, his Arctic route would start in Churchill, Manitoba, and go north along the west side of Hudson Bay. After a couple of relatively short overland traverses, he would pick up the fabled waterway at Spence Bay and follow it to Tuktoyaktuk. It took him three attempts and cost him most of his fingers and toes, but he did achieve his goal.

Early on, Starkell had said, "Polar bears are one of

my greatest fears." On his second attempt, in 1991, while camped on the Hudson Bay shore, Starkell had the opportunity of facing that fear. He was cooking seal meat on his stove when a polar bear picked up the enticing smell and came to investigate. The bear wanted the seal meat, and the man was in the way. The bear could have removed the human obstacle with one swipe, and judging by its single-minded approach, it intended to do so. Starkell ran at the bear, waving his arms above his head and shouting—and it worked. The bear looked confused and then ran away. Later, Starkell wrote of telling an Inuk the story. The Native remarked, "It was a pretty good thing to do. It might work once in a hundred times."

Farther north, near Wager Bay, where hundreds of seals gathered close to shore, so did the polar bears. Starkell saw at least four in one day and paddled in close to photograph a large lone male watching him from the land. The bear was about 80 yards away and was not initially perturbed when the unarmed Starkell foolishly growled at it. The bear moved closer, and the kayaker made his escape to sea, screaming and yelling at the bear as he did so. Had the bear been so inclined, it could have caught up with the kayak in a few seconds.

Don Starkell's adventures with polar bears did not end there. While he and his partner were paddling near Southampton Island, they were chased by a swimming polar bear. Starkell admitted that he had read how fast the bears could swim and for how far, but he hadn't really believed it. With a bear in hot pursuit in icy subarctic waters, he learned his lesson quickly and in graphic detail. The bear was fast. For longer than the kayakers expected, it powered through the water only a couple of kayak lengths behind them. That it was deliberately bent on attacking them was obvious. One error on behalf of either paddler would have enabled the bear to catch at least one of them, with tragic results. Fortunately, goaded by fear and by expending considerable effort, they were able to outdistance their pursuer.

9

Polar Bears in Fiction, Myth and Legend

DESPITE THEIR MYSTIQUE, OTHER THAN in a host of heavily illustrated children's books, polar bears have not enjoyed great stardom in fictional stories. Unfortunately, in illustrated children's books, polar bears are often shown interacting with penguins. That is a geographical impossibility, of course. Penguins only inhabit the southern hemisphere, in reasonable proximity to Antarctica, while polar bears are generally only found close to or north of the Arctic Circle (the major exception being the population in Hudson Bay). Adult fiction, even when centred on the Arctic, rarely features polar bears. There have, however, been a few interesting examples.

Although an often repeated story about a polar bear and Horatio Nelson, later to become famous as the Royal Navy hero

Admiral Lord Nelson, has been handed down as factual, it is almost certainly fiction. There is nothing in the log books of the voyage in question that suggests there is any truth in the story, and Nelson never mentioned it in any of his writings. However, it is worth repeating here because it is an interesting anecdote; if it was true, its hero almost did not reach the history books.

According to the story, at the age of 14, in 1773, Nelson was serving as a midshipman on a British warship, HMS *Carcass*, during a two-ship naval expedition to the Arctic commanded by Captain Constantine Phipps. The young Nelson was attacked by a polar bear while walking on the shores of Spitsbergen. Nelson tried to defend himself, but his musket misfired. Reportedly showing a glimpse of the bravery that would mark his long military career, he fought back against the bear by pounding at it with the stock of his useless weapon. Outclassed by a heavyweight and in imminent danger of a gruesome death, Nelson was saved when a booming report from one of the ship's guns sent the bear scurrying away across the snow for somewhere quieter.

British author Arthur Catherall wrote a short thriller for young adults about a polar bear that somehow found its way south to the Faroe Islands in the North Atlantic. The bear in that somewhat implausible tale, *The Strange Intruder*, created a brief reign of terror on the island before being trapped in a peat bog. There it was put to sleep with chloroform, caged and shipped off to a zoo.

The Welsh adventurer, sailor and author Tristan Jones

wrote of his encounters with polar bears in his 1978 book *Ice!* Whether these stories were true or not has never been proven. Jones was notorious for embellishing his exploits and, in some cases, inventing them outright. In the course of his literary career, he often cast himself in a truly heroic mold. His biographer (the author of this book) disproved many of the wily old sea captain's tales and showed that Tristan Jones' story of his lengthy sojourn in his boat in Greenland's ice was almost certainly fiction. Despite his questionable veracity, Jones wrote beautiful prose and exciting books. His first encounter with a polar bear, he wrote, was in September 1959.

According to his story, Tristan and his one-eyed, three-legged black Labrador, Nelson, were caught in Arctic ice just off the east coast of Greenland in their ketch, *Cresswell*. Jones opened the encounter with precision at the end of one chapter: "As I turned to go below, I saw the bear. Twelve feet long, padding silently, swiftly over the snow-laden ice. He was only fifty yards away, coming straight at the boat."

It is a dramatic set-up that guarantees the reader will turn the page to the next chapter. Tristan's story goes into high gear as the bear reaches the boat, stands up on its hind legs and begins tearing at the guardrails. The only weapons Tristan has are a harpoon and some emergency flares, plus the ever-valiant Nelson.

The heated battle between the bear and a man and his dog covers only three pages, but it is full of action. The bear stands upright and tears at the guardrails while Tristan jabs at it with a homemade harpoon, and Nelson snarls and barks. The bear is not intimidated. It rips the wire from the guardrail and bends the vertical iron stanchions as if they are made of putty. The bear gets its paws on deck, and Tristan stabs the harpoon through one of them. The bear rips the harpoon away while screaming in pain and anger. Nelson protects Tristan, and Tristan protects Nelson. The bear retreats to the ice and prowls around the boat, deliberately bumping hard at the hull with its shoulder.

Finally, Tristan goes below and loads a flare gun. The bear makes another attempt at getting on board, with Nelson trying his canine best to fight the monster off. Tristan returns to the deck and shoots a fiery flare into the bear's gaping mouth. It goes straight down his throat. In agony from the burning phosphorus inside, the bear falls backwards onto the ice and goes berserk, pounding the ice with its great paws and sending tremors through the boat and through Tristan. Nelson leaps onto the ice and attacks, but the bear has had enough. It plunges into the sea and vanishes. Tristan knows the bear cannot survive and return for a future attack, because the phosphorus from the flare will continue to burn inside the bear even when it is underwater.

Tristan Jones completes his fast-paced anecdote with details of how a polar bear stalks its prey across the ice, crouching low, moving slowly and keeping itself downwind—manoeuvres the Inuit employ and which Tristan himself adopts when he needs to hunt a seal later.

Although rarely written down, Inuit folklore is rich in tales that feature Arctic wildlife, particularly polar bears. Passed orally from generation to generation, most of the stories are quite violent, perhaps a reflection on the harshness of life in the Arctic. As is inevitable with oral storytelling, there are many variations of each story. The legend of Kaujjagjuak is a typical example. This is the simplest version.

Kaujjagjuak was a weak little orphan boy. He was also considered ugly because he had large nostrils. Although he lived in a small community, he had to survive alone because no one would take him in. He lived on whatever scraps of food he could find, usually discarded pieces of walrus hide. Almost everyone—men, women and children—abused Kaujjagjuak. The men of the village used to pick him up by his nostrils, take him into the singing house and make him take out the urine bucket.

The Man in the Moon watched the way people mistreated the boy and vowed to help him. He harnessed his dog to his sled and went down to Earth to meet Kaujjagjuak. At first the frightened boy refused to come out of hiding. When he did, the Man in the Moon carried him to a place known for its huge boulders. There, to the boy's surprise and pain, the Man in the Moon whipped him, saying it was to give him strength. After several whippings, Kaujjagjuak was bigger and very much stronger. The weak little boy had grown until he could pick up the boulders with ease.

On the next day, the Man in the Moon tested the mettle

of the villagers and Kaujjagjuak by sending three polar bears into the community. The village men lacked the courage to come out of their houses; only Kaujjagjuak was unafraid. He attacked the bears, killing two of them. The third bear he took back to the village and helped it kill some of the people who had treated him so badly when he was small and weak. Kaujjagjuak became a great hunter and travelled far and wide throughout the land.

A polar bear is the star of one major scene in a convoluted and long-winded story about a man named Kiviuk. After fighting a wild storm in his kayak, Kiviuk made his way to land and saw a stone house with a light in a window. He went inside and asked the owner, an old woman named Arnaitang, to dry his boots and slippers over her fire. Arnaitang, who had supernatural powers, agreed and let him stay. She was hoping to kill Kiviuk and eat him, but Kiviuk also had supernatural powers.

Once his footware was dry, Kiviuk reached up for them, but the drying rack over the fire moved out of his grasp. He called to Arnaitang for help, but she just said, "Keep trying." Kiviuk then understood that he was in danger. To protect himself, he called on his spirit helper, a large polar bear. The bear roared its disapproval from deep under the floor of the house, the sounds getting louder as the bear got closer. Arnaitang heard the bear and was afraid. She ran to Kiviuk and handed him his boots and slippers. And so Kiviuk was saved by a bear and was able to return to the sea in his kayak.

In some Arctic and subarctic regions, after killing a polar bear, the Inuit placed an arbitrary embargo on bears and would not hunt another for five days after killing a female and four days after taking a male. The Inuit believe that all creatures have souls and should be respected. They have a particular reverence for polar bears. The spirit of any creature in the animal world could be chosen as the spiritual guardian, or *tornaq*, of an individual. At the top of the *tornaq* hierarchy, the most powerful being of all is Sedna, the Goddess of the Sea. The polar bear is second only to Sedna.

If a hunt goes wrong, wounding a polar bear could create serious trouble for the hunter involved. The Inuit's traditional beliefs demand that a wounded bear be tracked down and killed, otherwise its soul will be deeply offended and bring sickness or other harm to the one who caused it unnecessary suffering.

Indigenous peoples on all continents have stories about the origins of the sun, moon and stars. The Inuit are no exception, and the polar bear has a special place in their skies. Inuit legends tell us that Nanuq, the polar bear, was chased off the world and into the sky by a pack of sled dogs. Nanuq and the dogs became the collection of stars that we know as the Pleiades, in the constellation of Taurus. They shine their light, as perhaps they should, close to the stars that make up Orion, the hunter.

10

Polar Bear Conservation

THE FIRST CONSERVATION PROJECTS INITIATED by the Wildlife Conservation Society Canada (WCS Canada) took place in the early years of the 20th century. Today, a century later, WCS Canada continues to work hard to fulfill its goals. Part of WCS Canada's stated mission is to "save wildlife and wild places in Canada by developing a better understanding of critical wildlife issues, designing science-based conservation solutions, and working with others to meet critical conservation objectives."

WCS Canada acknowledges that "the race is now on to safeguard the wild places and wild animals that still thrive in Canada." It is a race against time, but WCS Canada is not alone.

In 1973, the International Agreement for the Conservation of Polar Bears and their Habitat was signed by Canada, Denmark/Greenland, Norway, the former Soviet Union and the United States. Its purpose was to coordinate the overall management of polar bears in the wild. At the heart of the agreement, which is still in force, is the need to stop the decline in polar bear populations and to conserve the natural habitats within the bears' circumpolar range. It was further intended to safeguard the traditional hunting of polar bears by indigenous peoples around the Arctic. Part of the agreement directs all signatories to conduct ongoing research into management of polar bear populations within their areas and to exchange ideas, advice and information on conservation of the animals.

A few land areas have been set aside by concerned governments for the purpose of protecting the polar bears' habitat. The largest such areas are in the state of Alaska and Canada. The Arctic National Wildlife Refuge, which spreads across the state's north slope, is the singularly most important denning region for polar bears in Alaska; however, no part of the refuge has been set aside strictly for polar bear protection. Already, oil and gas concerns are clamouring for the north slope to be opened up for further development.

Canada has established two large areas for polar bear protection and several smaller ones. The two large areas are, perhaps strangely, far south of the Arctic Circle in the southern half of Hudson Bay. Although these two wilderness parks are the closest to heavily populated areas, they protect up to 2,000 bears between them. The two parks are Wapusk National Park, which stretches from just south of Churchill, Manitoba, to the Ontario border, and Polar Bear Provincial Park, which is wholly in Ontario. Wapusk is the Cree word for white bear, and the park is an important denning area for females. Covering 4,430 square miles of lowland tundra and taiga, it is home to 44 species of mammals, including a wild herd of 3,000 caribou and, of course, over 1,000 polar bears.

Ontario's Polar Bear Provincial Park was established to take care of the world's most southerly polar bear population, which congregates at the foot of Hudson Bay and into James Bay. Like Wapusk, its neighbour to the northwest, Polar Bear Provincial Park is a wilderness area with limited facilities for visitors.

The smaller regions where polar bears are protected include 5 national wildlife areas, all in Baffin Bay and Lancaster Sound, and 11 national parks of varying sizes. They can be found in 7 of the known subpopulation areas for polar bears: at the northernmost tip of Ellesmere Island, in the west on the Beaufort Sea coast of the Yukon, and in the east on Baffin Island. The most southerly area is Wapusk, on the west side of Hudson Bay. In addition, there are two marine protected areas, found in Newfoundland and Labrador in the Davis Strait subpopulation area. To add to that list, there are 58 provincial and territorial parks, which are located primarily in southern Hudson Bay, Foxe Basin and Davis Strait. To date, no other country can equal Canada's commitment to

An unusual image of a polar bear with snow-covered trees in the background. MILA ZINKOVA

polar bear conservation. Norway has, however, set aside Kong Karls Land (part of Spitsbergen) because of its large polar bear population and its importance as a denning site and has banned all human access. In other parts of the archipelago, especially in national park areas, travel restrictions are in force to reduce the impact of humans on the polar bear habitats.

Denmark and Greenland allow hunting by indigenous peoples but have yet to establish any dedicated conservation areas in Greenland. Russia, the largest country of the former Soviet Union, has no conservation areas for polar bears, and there are serious concerns by scientists in that country that poaching is causing irreparable harm to the polar bear population.

A report issued by the Ontario Ministry of Natural Resources in December 2008 stated in part: "The status of polar bear populations in Canada was reassessed in May 2008. The updated COSEWIC [Committee on the Status of Endangered Wildlife in Canada] report incorporates more community and Aboriginal Traditional Knowledge about polar bears. Elsewhere, in May 2008, the United States Fish and Wildlife Service listed polar bears as 'threatened' under the *United States Endangered Species Act*. Globally, the International Union for the Conservation of Nature (IUCN) listed the polar bear as 'vulnerable' in the IUCN Red List of Threatened Species."

On July 8, 2010, the premier of Manitoba announced that a $31 million International Polar Bear Conservation Centre would be established at the Assiniboine Park Zoo in Winnipeg. According to the premier, the facility is scheduled to be completed by the end of 2010 and will feature "a rehabilitation area for orphaned polar-bear cubs with a research, academic and public-education centre."

Outside government ministries, other organizations such as the World Wildlife Fund for Nature (WWF), Polar Bears International and International Fund for Animal Welfare (IFAW) continue their efforts to educate people about the need for polar bear conservation in particular and all wild creatures in general.

We can only hope those efforts are not too late and are not in vain.

The Inevitable Fate of Polar Bears?

AS THE WORLD CONTINUES TO warm up, the two polar ice packs melt and recede farther each summer. The ice-free months last a few days or a few weeks longer each year. Although there are two poles, only the Arctic ice cap directly affects polar bears. There, where once bears could roam and hunt for food on drifting ice all summer, the seas are more and more open. The ice becomes less and less. The bears have to work harder, travel farther and fast for longer between meals.

Eventually, if the north polar sea ice continues to melt at the same rate, the polar bears will have nowhere to go but the Arctic islands and the great land masses of the North. They will almost certainly move south as well.

Wherever they travel, they will inevitably encounter and provoke mankind into acts of violence. If nature's dwindling resource of ice does not directly cause the polar bear's extinction, mankind will eventually eradicate the bear populations for its own perceived safety—and the world will be so much poorer for the loss of yet one more valuable and eminently fascinating species.

In the summer of 2008, *ScienceDaily,* a popular and well-written Internet website, reported that scientists had recently conducted an aerial search of the Chukchi Sea off the coast of northwest Alaska and were concerned to discover a total of nine polar bears swimming far from land in open water. One was a full 60 miles from shore. With no ice nearby from which to hunt or on which to rest, that bear was in serious danger of exhausting itself and drowning, as were all the others too far from land or ice.

Discussing the lack of ice off Alaska's Arctic shores, Professor Richard Steiner of the University of Alaska's Marine Advisory Program was reported to have said, "The bottom line here is that polar bears need sea ice, sea ice is decaying, and the bears are in very serious trouble. For any people who are still non-believers in global warming and the impacts it is having in the Arctic, this should answer their doubts once and for all."

Selected Bibliography

Couture, Pauline. *Ice: Beauty, Danger, History.* Toronto: McArthur & Co., 2004.

Cowper, David Scott. *Northwest Passage Solo.* London: Seafarer Books, 1993.

Dalton, Anthony. *Baychimo: Arctic Ghost Ship.* Surrey: Heritage House, 2006.

———. *Arctic Naturalist: The Life of J. Dewey Soper.* Toronto: Dundurn Group, 2010.

Ellis, Richard. *On Thin Ice: The Changing World of the Polar Bear.* New York: Knopf, 2009.

Freuchen, Peter. *Vagrant Viking: My Life and Adventures.* London: Victor Gollancz, 1954.

Frison-Roche, Roger. *Hunters of the Arctic.* Toronto: Ryerson Press, 1969.

Horwood, Harold. *Bartlett: The Great Canadian Explorer.* Garden City, NY: Doubleday Co., 1977.

Jones, Tristan. *Ice!* Kansas City: Sheed, Andrews and McMeel, 1978.

Madsen, Marius. *Shipwreck and Struggle.* Toronto: Pitt Publishing, 1953.

McClure, Robert Le Mesurier. *The Discovery of the North-West Passage.* Edmonton: Hurtig, 1969.

Nansen, Fridjtof. *Farthest North.* London: Harper, 1898. Reprint, New York: Random House, 1999.

Norris, Stefan, Lynn Rosenstrater and Pål Martin Eid. *Polar Bears at Risk.* Gland, Switzerland: WWF-World Wide Fund for Nature, 2002.

Poulsen, Else. *Smiling Bears*. Vancouver: Greystone Books, 2009.

Pryde, Duncan. *Nunaga: Ten Years of Eskimo Life*. New York: Walker & Co., 1971.

Simon, Alvah. *North to the Night*. Camden, ME: International Marine Publishing, 1998.

Stefansson, Vilhjalmur. *My Life with the Eskimo*. New York: Macmillan, 1913.

Tyson, Captain George E. *Arctic Experiences*. New York: Cooper Square Press, 2002.

Vaeth, J. Gordon. *To the Ends of the Earth*. New York: Harper & Row, 1962.

Wood, Daniel. *Bears*. Vancouver: Whitecap Books, 1995.

Index

Acknowledgements

My initial thanks must go to Mark Ingebrigtsen, Mike Macri and Steve Miller—all from Churchill, Manitoba. To assist my search for polar bears some years ago, Mark loaned me his truck to follow the roads around Churchill; Mike took me out in his jet boat, *Sea North II*, and later in an inflatable speedboat. We watched beluga whales, seals and caribou, and we talked for hours. Steve Miller flew me far and wide over tundra and sea in his helicopter, skimming over drifting ice and barren coastal lands. Your time and your efforts are much appreciated. Equally, far away on the west coast of Alaska, in the remote village of Kivalina, my friends Chester Bundy and Sylvester Swan told me about the Arctic bears and their habits.

My family, most notably Penny and Pam, have always been supportive of my literary projects. They have my love and my thanks. Among my friends, Steve Crowhurst has always shown great enthusiasm for my books, as have Graeme Halley, Bill MacNeil, Bernice Lever, and more recently, Bill Hay.

Without the generosity and expertise of the staff of Heritage House, many of my books would not have been published. I am especially indebted to Rodger Touchie and Vivian Sinclair for their continued support, and to my ever-patient editor for this series, Lesley Reynolds. It is my pleasure to work with you.

About the Author

Anthony Dalton is the author of nine non-fiction books and co-author of two more, many of which are about the sea or about ships and boats. These include *The Graveyard of the Pacific*, *A Long, Dangerous Coastline*, *Baychimo: Arctic Ghost Ship* and *Alone Against the Arctic*, all published by Heritage House. Anthony is the national president of the Canadian Authors Association and is currently working on a book about shipwrecks of the Hudson's Bay Company for Heritage House's *Amazing Stories* series. He divides his time between homes on the mainland and in the Gulf Islands of British Columbia.

More Amazing Stories by Anthony Dalton

The Graveyard of the Pacific
Shipwreck Tales from the Depths of History

(ISBN 978-1-926613-31-4)

The magnificent west coast of Vancouver Island is renowned for its rugged splendour, but the coastline known as the Graveyard of the Pacific is haunted by the ghosts of doomed ships and long-dead mariners. These true tales of disastrous shipwrecks and daring rescues are a fascinating adventure into West Coast maritime history.

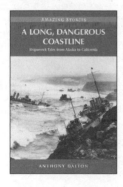

A Long Dangerous Coastline
Shipwreck Tales from Alaska to California

(ISBN 978-1-926613-73-4)

From San Francisco's Golden Gate to the Inside Passage of British Columbia and Alaska, the west coast of North America has taken a deadly toll. Here are the dramatic tales of ships that met their end on this treacherous coastline—including *Princess Sophia*, *Queen of the North* and others—and the tragic stories of those who sailed aboard them.

Visit heritagehouse.ca to see the entire list of books in this series.

Also in the Amazing Stories Series

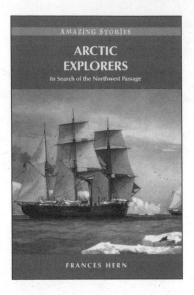

Arctic Explorers

In Search of the Northwest Passage

Frances Hern

(ISBN 978-1-926613-29-1)

The search for the Northwest Passage is a saga of hardship, tragedy and mystery. For over 400 years, the elusive, ice-choked Arctic waterway has been sought and travelled by daring men seeking profit and glory but often finding only a desperate struggle for survival. Spanning the centuries from Elizabethan privateer Martin Frobisher to RCMP officer Henry Larsen, the intrepid captain of the *St. Roch*, these stories of high adventure reveal why the Northwest Passage has gripped the imaginations of generations of explorers and lured them to its treacherous waters.

Visit www.heritagehouse.ca to see the entire list of books in this series.